About the Book

"There is a fine line between love and obsession, and on the map of our hearts that place may be marked by water – it is where we moor our wooden boats. Clinton Trowbridge, I suspect, knows that place well.... [A] charming memoir...frequently hair-raising and often funny."
                              –Mary Grace Butler, *Wooden Boat*

"I was taken by the writer's deft and engaging prose. Trowbridge has a way of hooking his reader.... Even land-lubbers like myself get caught up in the story.... He casts a writer's eye over his surroundings, bringing them to life."
                    –Carl Little, *Working Waterfront/Inter-Island News*

"You cannot help but be entranced by the great good fortune that allows this man and his marvelous boat to glide from mishap to disaster to mishap, quite without consequence."
                                        –John Cole, *Maine Times*

"The charm of this 192 page collection of family memoirs of experience over 26 years with an old 34' catboat is that it chronicles a lifestyle.... Clinton Trowbridge writes wonderfully well about all those years."
                              –Bob Hicks, *Messing About in Boats*

"Trowbridge writes eloquently of his love for Maine. His description of his arrival in Casco Bay after the cruise from New Jersey will resonate with any cruiser who has ever awakened to a new day on the water."
                                  –Sandy Marsters, *Points East*

THE BOAT THAT WOULDN'T SINK

Clinton Trowbridge

The Vineyard Press
Port Jefferson, NY

Preface

As I look back at the early fifties, when we bought the Scatt II, the boat described in these pages, what sticks out is the remarkable innocence of the times. Youth always thinks it will live forever, but not usually with such conviction and such consequent abandon. What seems foolish to the point of madness now, was then just a bit of derring-do. Beau Geste was our role model, and Swallows and Amazons our idea of a seafaring adventure. Nothing really bad could ever happen, and if we got into trouble, somehow we would get out. There were no sharks in the sea, and a wooden boat would always float.

One might think that only seven years after the end of the Second World War, life would have seemed less benign. I had but narrowly escaped both WW II and the Korean War, yet not only was I somewhat regretful of not having been involved, I—we—still managed to romanticize the experience of war itself. We flew with Chennault's Tigers and rode alongside Patton in his tank liberating the oppressed. America had not seen the miseries of war close up, not at home, and even our returning war heroes, like Audie Murphy, didn't want to talk about them.

We owned the Scatt for twenty-six years, however. She brought up the next generation and shaped all of our lives—taught us through example sometimes more than we wished to learn. The Scatt endured, more in spite of than because of us. And if we did too, that was partly her work as well. We grew closer to each other, and more alike—like ancient dogs and their masters.

This is a love story, then; and like all love stories, there is a strong element of nostalgia. Would that...could that... But we can't—and we don't really want to. It is also a book about joy, and sadness, and the thrills and perils of the sea. But most of all, it is a book about innocence: the life we imagine when we think of ourselves as gods.

PART ONE

THE CRUISE

1

Undampable Enthusiasm

The only time to buy an old, leaky, thirty-four foot wooden catboat is when you're young and don't know any better. We spent two weeks restoring the mahogany trim to glossy perfection, and ignored the three clean breaks in the keel. No one encouraged us to, and we didn't investigate what lay behind that patchwork of lead sheathing on the hull. We hammered it down, painted it over, and fondled the varnished spokes of the wheel instead, imagining hurricanes.

"Don't take her out of the bay." That was our neighbor's counsel. "Sail her to Maine? What'll you do if she opens up on you?"

It sounded exciting. We even knew that for the past few years—ever since she had been rammed head-on into a bridge piling during a storm—she had functioned primarily as a floating cocktail lounge, the host pumping, his wife salvaging guests from the briny deep; but that merely seemed romantic. We would save her, put her back into service. There was a six-foot splice in her mast, but when we heard how she had broken it—while sailing off the Jersey coast watching the Mauritania go down—we oohed and aahed and imagined ourselves saving lives at sea.

When all our work was done and they lowered her into the water to let her swell up and she filled in two hours, even then we were not bothered by gloomy thoughts. They pulled her out again, and two men spent a day boring holes, seemingly at random, into her timbers, which they filled with putty. We marveled at their ingenuity. We were ready to sail around the world when they put her in again and she leaked only moderately. If you pumped for ten minutes or so every few hours, you could keep even with the flow. After all, what did we expect for six hundred dollars?

We'd been married for a little over two years and had seven hundred dollars in the bank. The figure itself seemed auspicious; just what we could afford.

We were staying with Lucy's mother in Mantoloking, New Jersey, and were about to go to Maine to spend the rest of the summer with my parents. Why not sail there? It was nearly four hundred miles, but most of it was fairly protected. It seemed such a coincidence; there was the Scatt and here were we with more than enough money to buy her. She seemed to be waiting, cradled in that shipyard in Mantoloking as if under a Christmas tree for us to take her. A cruising boat! The cockpit was as big as a small room. Eight people could sit in it comfortably. The cabin slept four. Looking ahead from the wheel, I found myself caught in visions that I could never have resisted and remained myself. And Lucy loved the Scatt as much as I did. We hardly even talked about it. We put down the money in a sort of fog. It was only after we got back to Lucy's mother's house that we thought of all the reasons for how wise we had been.

There were moments of doubt but never any real loss of faith. After all, if worst came to worst, we could sell her piece by piece and make a profit. The lead on her keel would bring so much a pound, and what about that stainless steel rigging and those six, foot-long silvery turnbuckles? There were at least a dozen pulleys, some of which actually worked: collector's items, probably. Some yacht club would give us a fortune for that flagpole of a mast, or we could always sell it to the telephone company. There was a marine toilet, as well as four six-inch thick, specially made foam rubber mattresses to cover the two long bunks; they looked almost new and must have cost two hundred and fifty dollars at least. The wheel had actually been taken off an old clipper ship, we were told. Probably one hundred dollars right there anytime we needed the money; a real find.

However, even I could see that the engine would not bring very much. It squatted there in the bilge, one great flaking mass of rust. They did get it going for us, but it never really interested me. It worked occasionally. Hitting it with a hammer seemed to help. "Red" Kellog, the previous owner, told us that a man had offered him nine hundred dollars for the Scatt over the phone that morning and that we were sure lucky to have gotten in ahead of him with the money. After we signed the papers, he threw in the rest of a coil of quarter-inch Manila rope that he had in his basement. We took it but felt a little guilty robbing him blind like this.

Everything about the Scatt was about twice as big as we expected; it was two boats for the price of one. Her rudder was four feet long. It took six men to carry out her hollow, fifty-foot mast, and when they lowered it into place, we thought for a minute that her bow was going under. The sail weighed at least a hundred pounds, and we spent most of one day tying that huge piece of faded and patched canvas to boom and gaff and mast hoops. It looked like the mainsail of a seventy-foot schooner. There were miles of rope. It was a feat just to remember all the names: lazyjacks, topping lift, throat halyard, peak halyard, flying backstays. The mainsheet alone was two hundred feet long. We wouldn't get much for the rope, either, I guessed as I tried to sort one gray tangle from another. The sail, though. What a great circus tent.

2

Maiden Voyage

"Yes. Thanks. Just cast it off. Pull that line in, will you, Lucy? That one in the water." We are backing out of the slip: the wind is gusty and blows our stern up against the float on our right. Forward a little. Turn the rudder into the wind. Reverse. There, that's better.

"Watch out for the dinghy. It's slipped around!" cries our neighbor. Crunch. Sounds of splintering wood. Forward again. Hard to the left. The six-foot plywood dinghy that we have just paid twenty-five dollars for sweeps past the stern, and I see that, miraculously, only one side of it has been damaged. A few ribs, a little gluing and she'll be all right again.

Finally, we're away from the float and out into the channel. Having never sailed anything over nineteen feet, I have the sense that I'm taking out the Queen Mary. We motor out, into the wind at first. Unlike my parents' sloop in Maine, the Scatt seems totally unaffected by wind. We chug steadily up to the end of a line of slips, moving as placidly through the water as if on a bus. I turn the wheel to the left and we start a smooth arc that suddenly becomes much sharper as the Scatt sweeps too far down toward some pilings. Too late I turn the wheel back, and we grind a line of barnacles off the wooden piling that stands at the end of the slip. It recoils from our blow and throws us back toward the channel. The wind. I had no idea the wind would affect us that much as soon as we turned our side to it. I feel for the first time the massiveness of the Scatt. My impulse is to try to stop, but I realize that what we need is more

11

speed and push the throttle up a little. I am annoyed when I see our neighbor's smile and hear him calmly reassuring my mother-in-law and our friend, Taylor, who is up from New York to sail with us. "It's just a scratch. These boats are hard to handle." The Scatt is twice as wide as a racing sloop this length would be—fourteen feet—and full of majesty. Looking forward from the wheel, I have the illusion that beyond that huge mast there is another, smaller one, and that she really is a schooner. As we move down the middle of the channel, heading for the entrance to the bay, I swell with Toad-like pride. This boat, this ship, this magnificent vessel is ours, and we are going to sail her to Maine in a few days.

As we come out into the bay, we begin to pitch up and down a little. Immediately the Scatt feels lighter. With each downward plunge she smashes a counter wave fifteen feet off to each side of her bow. It's like driving through deep snow in a powerful car, or what I imagine it must be like in the engine house of a train, one of those old-fashioned ones with cow catchers on them, roaring through the snowy plains of the Dakotas or Nebraska. Only the motion is so graceful, up and down, as if on springs. There are whitecaps all over the bay, and across it, to the southwest, dark clouds tangle with the blue of the sky and move slowly toward us.

"Clint, why don't we just motor up to the house? You can try the sail when it's a nice, calm day," says my mother-in-law, somewhat hysterically.

"Good idea. No need to rush things," echoes our neighbor. Middle-aged-banker-on-the-Jersey-shore advice. Doesn't he know how exciting this is? What'll it be like when the wind catches that huge sail and the Scatt starts to heel over? How fast will she go? Will she be harder to steer? Will she tip much? Will her mast break? Will she leak worse than she does already? Will she open up and sink before we can get close enough to shore to jump off? These thoughts do not occur to me.

"She'll be all right," I say, and then to Lucy, shouting because of the wind, "Okay. Get ready with the sail." Taylor is standing by at the throat halyard, willing if able. "Slowly, now, keep together!" We have practiced this routine at the slip. It is a little tricky. The idea is to keep the twenty-five-foot gaff roughly horizontal as it goes up the mast. It's a little like hauling up a painter's scaffolding. It is hard to see what you're doing, though, with the sail slashing all over the place. "More on your end, Taylor," I yell, and the base of the gaff jerks up another few feet until it is even with the tip. "Together, now, faster." About half of the sail is up and the wind is raking the boom back and forth across the deck like a guillotine. I have to keep ducking my head. The "oldies" are crouched, heads down, in the far left corner of the cockpit. Taylor is kneeling on the floor waiting for instructions.

"Just keep pulling," I say. Now they both pull together, and finally Taylor's end is up and he wraps the rope around the cleat and sinks to the floor. Lucy pulls the tip of the gaff as high as it will go, and it's done. It seems to have taken hours.

The sail begins to fill and we heel to starboard. We tip more and more and I hear Lucy's mother groaning, realize that we're sailing too far downwind and let the wheel go; but instead of coming up, the Scatt keeps on the way she is. She is sailing sideways, and I have to brace my right foot against the lower seat to keep from falling. I look behind me to see if by any chance the rudder has fallen off, and then our neighbor reminds me that we have forgotten to lower the centerboard.

Luckily the engine is still running. I bring the Scatt up into the wind, and Lucy pushes the centerboard down with the mop handle. We fall off again and this time we shoot forward. The lee rail is almost under. I pull in the mainsheet a little more and look up at the smooth belly of the sail as it stretches out over half the sky. The rigging, all those ropes which were so hard to figure out before, looks simple and beautiful from here, a crisscross of lines stitching the gaff loosely to the top of the mast with little balloons between each of the mast hoops, but no real sags. The three lines of reef points jingle in unison, like tinsel on a Christmas tree. The rail is under now. Each dip of the bow sends spray back as far as the cockpit. It flies over my mother-in-law's head. She is moving cautiously toward the cabin, but I am taking in so many other things that I do not pay much attention to her turtle-like motions. I stand in order to hold the wheel more securely. The water rolls six feet, at least, out from under the raised stern.

"Clint! We're sinking!" cries my mother-in-law. She is standing in water up to her ankles. One of the floorboards has come loose and is floating around.

"Taylor," I shout, "can you get the pump going?" Taylor looks somewhat shaken up, but he maneuvers his way into the cabin, gets out the rusty, galvanized hand pump and steadies it up against the centerboard well. "We haven't pumped her in at least half an hour," I say in a voice that seems to reassure Lucy, at any rate.

"You'd better lower the sail and motor in," says our neighbor. "The strain's too much for her. And if you want my advice, you won't take her out of the..." I'm beginning to hate our neighbor. Mama Reeves is edging her way out past Taylor, and finally collapses back into the corner of the cockpit.

I look below. Taylor is pulling at the pump handle with a resigned sort of ferocity, but he doesn't seem to be making much of an impression on the bilge. "Okay. I guess you're right," I say. "Prepare to lower the sail." I press the starter button. Nothing. A buzz. The key is on. I try again. Same buzz.

"Better just sail her back," growls Big Jowls. "She won't leak as much going with the wind. Be lucky if your engine's not ruined."

"Ready about. Hard a lee!" I toss out the orders grimly. The maddening old killjoy. Nagging, nagging.

"Get your head down, Lucile! It's all right. We'll

be home in a little while."

We come roaring up into the wind and then we're over on the other tack and I'm letting the sail out. Things are suddenly much quieter. The mooring in front of Lucy's mother's house is about a quarter of a mile away, and we are headed right for it. We're going much faster than I expected. It takes all my strength to hold down the wheel. Suddenly we are planing, shooting down the slope of a wave, yet caught, timeless, within the wave itself, its white foaming lip riding alongside of us, buoying us up, lifting us into itself as it surges on and on and on. What ecstasy! No one else seems to notice.

Lucy and Taylor are bailing with buckets into the cockpit. The water drains out the self bailing holes too slowly for our neighbor and he bails it directly overboard. Lucy's mother still looks terrified, but then she has some kind of phobia about water. She was on the Titanic, as she's often told us, and she never liked boats much to begin with. Now that we are nearing the house, though, she looks a little less certain that she is going to drown. She inches over toward me on the seat, the knuckles of both hands showing white as she clutches the cockpit railing with what appears to be a superhuman act of courage, and fastens her grip on my left forearm. Fixing me with her Ancient Mariner stare, she says, "Promise me one thing. That you won't take Paul along."

Lucy hears this urgent pleading and we exchange looks. Not take Paul? What does she mean by saying such a thing? And if she is so afraid, why doesn't she beg us not to go? Leave our year-old baby behind? She must be mad.

3

Paul

We have constructed a bamboo and rope play-pen-crib for Paul in the forward section of the starboard bunk. Already he has learned how to crawl out of this cage. But it doesn't matter. The cabin is his giant play-pen. Sailing along, thinking he is sleeping, we are surprised to see his face at the stairs. Or we hear splashing sounds and gurgles of baby pleasure, and know it is time to pump. I am sure he has already learned the word "water" ("wawa"), though Lucy disagrees. I imagine him developing a premature and strictly marine vocabulary in the next few weeks and am quick to read his burbles and grunts as the first indications of a remarkable linguistic ability. He loves the motion of the Scatt, squeals with delight when his combination potty-highchair slides him back and forth across the floor of the cockpit in a good sea. The first day we have him on board, he takes his nap on the rubber doormat in front of the cabin steps. He sleeps with his knees under his fat belly, his bottom raised to the sun.

Mama Reeves has resigned herself to grandchildlessness and given us her reluctant blessing. With Taylor and myself this takes the form of absurd and expensive yachting caps, real ones, with the appropriate naval titles, captain and first mate, as if this assertion of rank will protect us from disaster. We assume that the last few weeks have slightly unhinged her, so we humor her and wear them. Soon we grow to like them, feel as if somehow we are nearer the sources of command, the wells of knowledge, when we have them on. Like the actor who believes he cannot perform well unless he wears certain favorite shoes, we find ourselves strengthened by appearances.

The Scatt leaks only normally when we sail her with the wind, and it reassures Mama Reeves somewhat to learn that "down east" means "down wind." "We'll hug the coast all the way," I promise and to comfort her still more, add, "We can always just crash her ashore and jump off if we have to." A mistake. The image is too vivid.

Paul has developed a strong attachment for the Scatt. He cries whenever we take him off his boat, is pacified only when we push him back and forth across the living room floor in his potty-highchair. He wants to go sailing worse than any of us. When he is not playing in the "wawa," zooming back and forth in his chair, or sleeping on his mat, he curls up on one of the cockpit seats and stares out at the water, thinking deep thoughts. I am convinced that he thinks of the boat as his playmate. He pats the gray deck as if it were a dog, and laughs hysterically and without discrimination at everything the Scatt does. I am also sure that his vocabulary is already remarkable: "Dah?" (good, excited, said with great approval and apparent pride as the sail goes up), and "Dah!" (bad, disappointed, as the sail is lowered, but only mockingly so, as if this were our attitude; he knows that the sail will rise again). "DAH!" (spoken in tones of absolute wonder when the sail is full and doing its work).

Each time I try to teach Paul to say "Scatt," he says "caaat." He must think the Scatt and his grandmother's gray cat are in the same category. "Scatt" is simply "It's a cat." "Scatt," "cat" he pats the gray deck or pounds on the hatch of the purring motor. Imagine his confusion when he discovers that the Scatt is a catboat.

Already Paul can pull himself up by the spokes and stand at the wheel. His favorite nautical garb is an old heather-colored sweater of Lucy's. With my cap tilted rakishly over his head and his sunburnt, diaperless bottom just showing, he stands there wobbling drunkenly, shouting "DAH!" at the top of his lungs. He adores sitting on my lap as I steer, his hands on mine. He stands, or sits behind the wheel, shouting orders to the crew, commenting on everything: the jovial, garrulous captain of a Walt Disney kiddy adventure story. I am beginning to worry that it may prove impossible to readjust him to life on shore when our voyage is over. And if he learns how to walk this month, will he stagger like a drunken sailor the rest of his life?

4

Taylor

Taylor has been having trouble adjusting to shipboard life. Though we have been taking trial runs in the bay for over a week, he still has not mastered the art of steering. "It's like a car," I tell him, forgetting that he does not drive. "If you turn the wheel to the left, the boat goes to the left." He makes the maneuver. "Fine. Now bring her back on course again." This seems to panic him for he turns the wheel still further to the left and looks betrayed when the Scatt starts to make a circle. "To the right. Turn the wheel to the right." We start circling the other way.

The problem is that he cannot seem to orient himself on the water, has no idea what a course is. "Just line up the mast with that bridge. Keep her going in that direction," I explain, losing hope as the Scatt weaves from side to side, Taylor squinting.

"What bridge?" he says. His vision is not the best. He needs something sticking out of the water, and not too far away, to guide him. A buoy. If he can see it, he can usually steer for a buoy, but only for a short time. It rattles him badly if the Scatt slips away even a little bit, and invariably he steers hard in the wrong direction to get her back on course again. Snake wake. Sea serpent wake. We sail in circles.

It doesn't seem possible, but in a week and a half he shows no improvement. By then he is convinced he will never learn. He speaks of steering as a talent and admires ours. So we drop it for the time being. Maybe it really is his eyesight, or something to do with the fluid in the inner ear, for he doesn't seem comfortable with the boat's motion, either.

If there are any waves, he lurches around, gripping railings. It's as if a man with two wooden legs has been impressed into a ballet troupe.

He is more at home with ropes. He and Lucy can raise the sail now in under a minute. If it's a flat calm, he can pull the anchor. What he likes to do, though, is to make rope mats. As soon as we are underway, he will find the end of the flying back stay or some other rope, place it on something solid—the deck, the cockpit floor—and wind the rest of the line around it with the twisting flat of his palm. The throat halyard—his rope, the rope he handles when we raise or lower the sail—makes a mat two feet across; and on the cockpit floor, in front of the varnished mahogany cabin doors, it does give, I have to agree, a regal yacht-like look to our continually sinking vessel. His best speed at doing this is fourteen minutes, but perhaps the length of time all this rope work takes is to the good, since it is something with which to wile away the long hours at sea. Like the yachting caps, these mats become symbols of our competence to get to Maine without disaster. When we lower the sail at the end of a day, Taylor looks wistful as his mat is destroyed, but each morning he rebuilds.

He doesn't care for pumping, but that is perhaps where he is most useful, propped up just inside the cabin doors, leaning against our six-foot galvanized hand pump, sloshing bilge water into the centerboard well, recycling the sea. We argue that it will build him up, all this exercise, that by the time we reach Maine he will be a regular Charles Atlas.

Actually, Lucy and I wonder if he should make the trip. We hint that he can duck out and not lose face, but in some way going is more important to him than to either of us. He insists that he will survive. Lucy and I have sailed small boats all our lives, but this is a first for Taylor. Even if it does not make him into a seaman, the experience is bound to do something for his writing. He is seeking metamorphosis. Did not Conrad and Melville go to sea? He will write about his adventures, he tells us. At the very least he will be able to keep the bookstore people with whom he works in New York amused with stories all winter. Also, it really takes three to handle the Scatt, and there is no one else free at the moment to sail with us. The first leg of the voyage is the forty-mile open stretch of sea from here to New York City. Today, Bay Head! Tomorrow, the world!

5

Rescue at Sea

July 1. It is just after eight o'clock and we are all on board ready to push off. It is cloudless, almost windless; already the heat is unbearable. We have been up since before dawn packing the interminable few last things, and we itch, we pant, to cut ourselves loose from this baking dock and all the niggling details of endless preparation. A five- to-ten-knot wind from the SE is predicted but there is no whisper of it yet. The conditions are almost too perfect. We could float to New York on rubber rafts on a day like this.

Lucy's mother is, nevertheless, mildly hysterical. Our neighbor, for once, speaks on our side. "It couldn't be a better day, Lucile. Let's just hope the weather stays like this," he says, and presents us with a package of distress flares. The present amuses us but undoes all his good work. Luckily, he gets most of the flak.

"They'll probably never use them. They're not planning to sail at night. It's just a precaution. Lucile, please! There's no need to..." The heat's on, though, and he sweats more than ever. We thank him. They will be great for the 4th.

I start the engine and we make ready to cast off. Though we have been saying goodbye almost without interruption for the past two days, only now does Lucy's mother seem to realize that the time has actually come. She focuses a last liquid eye on each of us in turn but to no avail. I promise her for the nth time that we will call at each spot our feet touch shore, and finally we are off: waving, waving, waving; heading for Manasquan Inlet and the open sea.

Though the surface of the water is glassy way

out to the horizon point, there are choppy swells in the narrow inlet and the Scatt takes her first noseful of sea water, her bow plunging under with each wave. She bucks, she prances, as if the bay had been her corral. She is free now to charge across the open plains of the sea. Standing up on the seat behind the wheel, draped casually over the boom, steering with my right foot, I breathe deeply of the fresh sea air, my nostrils flaring in sympathetic communion. I can hear things crashing around in the cabin, though, and at a look from Lucy I get off my perch and slow down the engine. The tide is with us and in a few minutes we are out of the breakers and riding easily on the swells. As we pass the break-water, I wave to the fishermen sprinkled here and there among the gulls and the seaweed-bearded rocks and beyond them to the thousands who lie or sit or walk upon the beach. We are taking leave of all of them, it seems; leaving; taking our leave: escaping, vanishing, voyaging. Faint ripples have disturbed the glassy surface of the water, and we put up the sail. By ten o'clock we are sailing lazily along with the wind a half mile off the cottage-crowded shore, heading for New York.

I am the one to suggest a swim, and turn the wheel over to Lucy. A shallow dive from the bow brings me up amidships, and I stroke over to the big blue hull but then change my mind and dive under the water to swim next to her. I love the way the Scatt's smooth belly submarines through the water. The three feet or so of protruding centerboard takes my eye down to the misty, and then dark, depths below me, and I come up for air, shivering. It is a little spooky, swimming in the ocean. One imagines being suddenly confronted by the cow-like eye of a giant tuna. There are swordfish in these waters, too. Sharks occasionally frighten the bathers along this coast, and then the beach is closed for a few days. I let myself fall back along the hull, more at ease if I stay on the surface, and then swim over to the rope that we are trailing and lie there, both arms extended out in front of my chest so that I seem to be planing. I adore this sensation of water slipping by my chest and thighs—the sense of motion, oneself motionless. I let the Scatt tow me, salmon-like, through the sea.

My face begins to dry in the sun, and I lie there gazing at the sail which fills the sky in front of me. The Scatt's stern looks massive from this angle. I feel shrunken in size and am more aware than ever of her majesty. The soft, hip-like curve of her hull encourages me to imagine that I follow in the wake of a queen. Lucy looks back at me and says, "Aren't you getting cold?" I shake my head, smiling at her, take a last dip under and then pull myself in, hand over hand, on the rope, almost losing my bathing suit.

"Go on in. The water's great."

Lucy hangs off the back of the boat and then plops down directly onto the rope with a little "oooh." I have done this before, in the bay, but she has not, and she pulls herself back to the boat almost right away. I help her in over the stern. She has had even more trouble with her bathing suit than I; she is a mermaid that I have angled up from the sea, her legs melted into one jeweled limb by the bubbly turbulence of the Scatt's wake.

"It's fun, but I think I like it better when we're stopped," she says.

Taylor is lying down on top of the cabin. "It'll make you feel better," I tell him. "Go on, there's nothing to it." Finally he jumps from the bow, way out, as if from the deck of a sinking ship. He goes so far down that when he reappears, he is behind the stern. Immediately his arms flail around for the trailing rope, but he is too far out. He does a few feeble strokes, in the wrong direction, and we both start yelling at him, but by the time he sees the rope it is too late and he is past its end. I bring the Scatt into the wind and Lucy throws over the air mattress. I push the starter but it doesn't catch, and we move further and further away from him until we cannot see him at all. Luckily, I can see the mattress, and I bring the Scatt around and sail for it. Finally, we glimpse his head about thirty feet from the mattress and, relieved, we yell out encouraging words.

He is white and as limp as a spent sturgeon when we pull him on board, prickled with goose flesh all over. We try to joke him out of his fear, but it has been real. He lies on the deck, exhausted, and says nothing. Finally, he groans. And then speaks. And we know he is all right, "Your mother and her nightmares!"

By now it is lunch time and we are famished. We dig at the contents of the larder, unearthing deviled ham, hard-boiled eggs, icy milk, Hydrox cookies and six gushy, droosly-soft purple plums. No food ever tasted so good. The wind has come up a bit and it is cooler. We skim along in a following sea at about four knots. In the distance, barely visible, is Sandy Hook. We see our first porpoises: smooth miniature whale-backs arching through the blue water at our side—the legendary lifeguards of the sea. The food, the wind, the day, the mild adventure behind us, the contentment of riding the waves on our floating island; all of this makes us sure that even better things are ahead.

But after lunch, with the air mattress for a dummy, we practice rescue at sea. I discover that an instant jibe will bring us back to within a few feet of the floating body. It would be dangerous to do in a high wind, but Taylor assures us that as far as he is concerned, it will not be necessary. He speaks of life lines, of tying himself to the mast. Only I, apparently, ever plan to swim at sea again, and then, Lucy tells me, only when we are barely moving.

6

Night Visitors

Verrazano is just a name to us. We know little about the great explorers and so can easily imagine ourselves in their company. Entering New York Harbor at sunset, teamed for a moment with a banana boat from Panama, we feel like seasoned voyagers. The Statue of Liberty holds out a rosy arm in welcome. The dying sun is reflected from a million Manhattan windows; the Chrysler building is a doge's palace.

To keep our illusions, we anchor half a mile or so offshore, opposite the Battery. A tugboat captain has told us that the tides will be slack at Hell Gate, up the East River, at nine o'clock, so we must be on our way by seven a.m. We are ready to turn in early anyway. It is exhausting sitting on a boat in the sun all day, we discover.

Before going to bed, I hoist the anchor light to the crosstrees after stuffing the hole in the glass with a tiny wad of toilet paper. I have trouble lighting it—the wick is ragged—but when it is up there with the stars, I am glad to see it. Though it looks no bigger than a firefly, it marks our spot. It is our night light and will comfort our sleep.

Taylor, over on his bunk next to Paul, wrestles for some time in search of a position tolerable for his sunburn, but the water lapping softly against the hull, an inch and a half beyond our ears, lulls us to sleep. In what must be no more than a few hours, the wind comes up and I wake to the slashing of ropes against the mast.

The Scatt is pitching from stem to stern and rolling violently. I reach over onto the floor and plunge my wrist deep into water. I get up and pump for fifteen minutes, until I am no longer standing in it. The whistling of wind in the rigging is steady but varies in pitch from a cowlike moan to the screeching of a tomcat. Lucy and Taylor are awake but they make only muffled and intermittent sounds. I am wide awake myself, cannot imagine sleeping. A downpour of rain sweeps over us, drumming hail-like on the cabintop. I look out the doors but can see nothing except a few tiny lights. I think of checking the anchor, but decide that it must be holding or we wouldn't be pitching so. I am up for about half an hour standing about, listening, wondering if I should do something. Finally, I get back into my end of the bunk.

Lucy mutters, "Everything all right?"

"I guess so. Just a squall."

There are damp spots on my blanket and an unpleasant drip near my head. I turn the pillow over and place it on the outer edge of the bunk. I lie there stiffly, hoping that nothing happens, trying to empty my mind for sleep. For hours, it seems, I lie there, unsuccessfully repelling the invading images that jolt my body to wakefulness. I try counting sheep, and suddenly they're waves crashing over me instead. What if it were really storming out? We will have to pick good, protected anchorages from now on, and tie up to a mooring whenever we can. The anchor line is heavy—one-inch manila—but not exactly new. Each heave the boat takes seems a strain I must bear as well, and I struggle to breathe. Where are those leaks coming from? I could tie the halyards to the mast and they wouldn't bang so. Should I get up and pump again? The rain squalls pass and there is less strain to our motion. The anchor line ceases to tug at me; the various sounds merge and begin to recede as if back down a dark tunnel, and finally I fall asleep. Paul has not made a sound.

* * *

"Who's captain here?"

I blink furiously in the strong light but cannot see who it is. "I am," I say quickly. "What's the matter?" I am out of bed and pulling on my pants.

"Get your riding light on! Lucky you haven't been run down. Don't you know you're in the shipping lane?"

I scramble up on deck and explain to the two Coast Guard men that I had put up a light, had no idea...

"See that it stays lit. Too late to move you now."

"Yes, I'll see to it. Thanks for telling us."

It's beginning to get light in the east. Soon it will be time to get up, I realize, as I watch the Coast Guard boat roar off toward Brooklyn. The sea is calm now, but I have to brace myself against the cabin as their wake hits us. The spires of Manhattan stand out in grim silhouette against the battleship gray of the sky. You wouldn't have a chance. Those sudden lurchings in the night—tugs? A tanker? How close had they come? How long has the light been out? I shake the lamp but cannot tell for sure how much kerosene is left. The wad of toilet paper is still there so I light it again and raise the lamp to the crosstrees where it flickers like some far-off star. I had never thought of our lives as depending on this tiny shimmer of light and vow to find out what the trouble is tomorrow. Today, I mean. Later today. There is the faintest trace of pink in the sky now, but I stagger back into the cabin to try for some more sleep before the day really starts. As I settle under the blanket, I realize, in disbelief, that our cruise to Maine is still in its first twenty-four hours.

7

Hell Gate

It seems only seconds later that I am awakened by Paul who is crawling over my head in search of his bottle. More welcome is the aroma of coffee and bacon, though most welcome would be more sleep. Taylor must have already pumped, I notice, as I swing my feet over onto dry boards. Everyone seems unpleasantly bright and cheery.

"Who were those men in the middle of the night?" says Lucy, pouring me some coffee.

"Coast Guard," I grunt. "Our riding light went out."

"We could have been run down?"

I grunt in the affirmative. Two eggs, bacon, fried-bread-toast, more coffee; it's another beautiful day. I begin to feel more human. Outside, I see that Taylor has transformed us into a laundry barge, the clothes already steaming. He calls my attention to the time: seven-ten, and I try the engine. Wunderbar! The gods are with us. Taylor pulls the anchor and we move out. The skyscrapers of Manhattan stand before us like grim sentinels. We have no time to lose and I give her full throttle, about five knots. Six tides meet at Hell Gate and I know it is essential for us to get there at slack water. I have seen them many times, the tugs, breasting the current, barely making headway against it as they force their way up the East River. The influx from the Harlem River moves even the tugs off course, and there are sluggish, ominous-looking whirlpools that only their locomotive engines and monstrous propellers can control. It is still one of my favorites, the East River Drive, one hundred and twenty-five blocks or more from the

Triboro to Fulton Street. Usually there are only the tugs, but sometimes there are more frail craft racing along with, or charging against, the bilious waters that float through the narrow trench that joins Long Island Sound and the Hudson, and divides Queens from the Bronx and Manhattan from Brooklyn: Manhattan, that tiny island in what must be the most putrid of seas; Manhattan, home of seven million. It would be fun to see ourselves, I think, as we pass into the mouth of the East River.

The still-rising tide helps us. If nothing goes wrong with the motor, we should be all right. There is no wind. I have to keep a sharp eye ahead to avoid the debris in the water: orange crates, chicken crates, planks, boxes of all shapes, barely floating timbers that look like telephone poles. Also the burgeoning sea traffic: pleasure boats flashing their "V"-shaped hulls at us as they pass to bow or stern on their way to the Atlantic, the ponderous hulk of the Staten Island ferry flying through the water at fifteen knots. An ocean liner is being inched out into the Hudson by two tiny bearded tugs, up past the Battery.

On the Brooklyn side, we pass wharf after wharf of rusty tramp steamers, their three-inch hawsers delicate filaments holding them spider-like to the shore. Though there is no wind, we are tossing about as if in a gale—a taste of what's to come. Lucy peers out of the cabin to see what's causing all the commotion. A man carrying an attache case is walking briskly along not thirty yards from us on the Manhattan side.

"People going to work!" she says and laughs as if in amazement that this were possible—people working, going to jobs. The man glances in our direction and she waves to him. He stops dead and stares at us, at her, and Lucy ducks back into the cabin again to get dressed.

We are approaching the Brooklyn Bridge and, though I know it is absurd, I look up at the tip of the mast to see if it will clear. From this angle you can't really tell. I resist the impulse to slow down—ridiculous!—but I have less faith in theory than in sight, and I cannot look as we go under. Part of me sees the wreckage already, hears the tearing, wrenching sounds of splintering wood. We hear wheels thundering overhead and are momentarily "exhausted." Another bridge almost right away, the grim, gray emptiness of the Navy yard, another bridge (I have stopped looking up now), and then, way off in the distance on our left, the oasis of the UN building, sparkling in the sun. As we approach Hell Gate, the state hospital on Wards Island looms into view, flanked by dismal-looking apartment houses.

Lucy emerges from the cabin dressed in white shorts and a blue sleeveless shirt. She gasps as a huge rat scurries along the lower timbers of a wharf not more than ten feet away. Some kids are swimming off the wharf next to it, pushing each other in, laughing and taking huge leaps into the air. A large tug is overtaking us on our right. We wave, and the captain waves back. The current has slowed to almost nothing. There are little eddies all around us, sucking at the debris; in the middle of one of them the bloated body of a cat circles slowly in a counter clockwise direction. Ant-like commuter traffic moves over the bridges from Queens. I do not think of Whitman or Hart Crane. I think mainly of nothing. My mind is too wrapped up in the moment to analyze its impressions.

There is gray scum along the Scatt's waterline. The froth kicked up by the propeller and carried along by us under our stern looks like the blackened soapsuds of a miner's wash day. One should feel like a Lilliputian taking his walnut shell boat up a sewer main, yet instead there is a "Ratty," a "Moley" sense of adventure about all this, as if we were successfully navigating the rivers of the underworld.

The waters at Hell Gate are against us when we get there, and we barely make it through. So narrow is the passage that we can see the faces behind the barred windows of the state institution on our left. The tide is still strongly against us as we pass the penitentiary on Rikers Island, but the East River broadens now into a bay and loses its strength. Like giant condors, the planes of La Guardia circle overhead, strafing us with their jet streams. But we are safe now. The Whitestone Bridge arches over us, Throgs Neck is just ahead, and beyond it are the ever-widening waters of the Sound.

8

Through the Sound

By ten o'clock a good breeze has come up from the SW and we raise the sail. We have seen other sailboats, but what lies before us now is a fleet: the armadas of Little Neck and Eastchester bays. A sixty-foot brigantine sails out past the point at Fort Totten and overtakes us, though we give her a good chase. Running like this with her sail way out to starboard, the Scatt has a tendency to come up into the wind, and I stand up behind the wheel to make the steering easier. She looks, and handles, like a lop-sided square rigger. This is why she has such a huge rudder, I realize, feeling the strain on my arms as I turn the wheel down to hold her straight, envying the brigantine her hermaphrodite rig, the huge square sail that pulls her easily past us. Most of the ordinary small sloops we can beat—not the big ones, with their great, bellying spinnakers, but the ones our size and under, with no extra sails. We wave as we sail past them.

The wind is maybe fifteen or twenty knots and Taylor is kept busy pumping. We are almost planing on the waves, but not quite. By noon we have passed New Rochelle and from there on the towns seem to flash by like stops on a commuter train: Larchmont, Mamaroneck, Rye, Greenwich, Stamford, Norwalk and finally Bridgeport, where we put in for the night. Fifty-some miles. We can hardly believe it.

Though I have had to relieve Taylor at the pump from time to time, we figure that the Scatt has been leaking only about twice as much as usual. It is her speed, though, that really impresses us. We could be in Maine in a week at this rate.

Bridgeport is a mistake; it's like going back into New York harbor only it's smaller and from no distance exotic. It is calm, however, though not quiet, and we find a mooring and after dinner locate a pay phone among the grimy docks and call Mama Reeves. There's a poor connection and it takes us most of the three minutes to explain to her where we are.

"No, Mother. Bridgeport, not Newport." She's impressed anyway. "Yes, fine. Paul is fine too. FINE! He LOVES it when it tips... NO, IT HARDLY TIPS AT ALL! BYE! Tomorrow night. TOMORROW NIGHT. IF WE CAN!"

We fall into bed at nine o'clock, and tonight we all sleep like babies. About six-thirty we are jostled awake by the noise and motion of the boat traffic around us, but that gives us an early start. It is the hottest day yet: in the nineties, humid and sticky even on the water. The motor abruptly stops about halfway out of the harbor, and for an hour we drift with the outgoing tide until I find the loose connection. Just looking at this filthy engine seems to cover me with grease. The fan belt has been loose for some time, apparently, and has fouled even the underside of the hatch with the fine black dust of vulcanized rubber. I feel more like a garage mechanic than a sailor. I hate this hulking, blackened, inarticulate beast that I cannot understand and that tries to turn me into something I am not and have no wish to be—but I am pleased with myself when I attach the loose wire and the motor starts. By then a slight breeze has come up from the SW and we put up the sail. I would give a lot to be able to plunge overboard and cool off—clean off—but the murky water does not look inviting. My fingerprints are everywhere, even on the sail.

We mosey along up the coast, and then the tide changes and we barely make any progress at all. Taylor is the only one in a good mood. Yesterday he hardly spoke after we got the sail up, and slept on the cabintop most of the afternoon. Today he chatters away and even reads aloud to us from his favorite author, Saki. I lie on the seat and steer with my right foot, wishing the wind would come up some more or stop entirely so I would be obliged to motor. I am superstitious about the engine and feel we should keep its power in reserve. Or maybe I simply dread the thought of having to wrestle with it again if it doesn't work. I want to go swimming, but even out here the water looks lifeless and dank. I catch an occasional word, but I am too lethargic, or uninterested in Saki to really listen.

Paul, who either slept or burbled with ecstatic joy—"dah! dah! dah!"—all day yesterday, whines and won't sleep and won't eat, and won't do anything, apparently, except make Lucy irritable. She goes in and out of the cabin continually—for something, with something, for nothing—as if the Scatt were her cage. Finally, she gets Paul to sleep and lies down herself on the bow, where the sail provides a spot of shade. Taylor is reading to himself.

There is nothing much to look at, no islands to sail between, nothing but an endless huddle of ugly houses and smokestacks on the shore. There are a few other sailboats but they sit like cut-outs on the water and seem hardly real. Outboards skim across the placid surface of this noxious pond like water beetles and remind us of our own immobility; or circle us, vulture-like, as if waiting for our death throes to cease. Tankers! Oil slick! We are practically underneath the traffic on the interstate. Only fifteen miles!

The next day is not much better, though with the help of the motor we make Old Saybrook, at the mouth of the Connecticut River, and enjoy the fireworks display at the town dock. Independence Day. Freedom. Maybe tomorrow we will feel free. Where is the wind?

The next day starts off the same—we are beginning to waste away with the tedium of it all—but at about five in the afternoon, just as we are trying to fix on a harbor for the night—West Mystic? Stonington?—the wind suddenly freshens and we decide to try for Point

Judith, thirty miles away. It will mean some night sailing but we are too eager to take advantage of the wind to worry about that.

The wind gets stronger as the sun sets, and the air has a sea nip in it. Ever since we passed Fishers Island the waves have been building up, and now they are white-crested and a good five feet high. We are almost planing in a wind that I estimate to be about twenty knots. I consider reefing but decide not to. A little more and we will lift into the air and shoot the rapids of these seas at eight or nine knots, but we don't quite make it. If I don't turn the wheel down fast enough, or if my hand slips on the polished varnish of the spokes, the Scatt gets away from me, angles down and then sails across the waves, the lee deck going under as she tilts her hull up into the wind's face. This delights Paul, who immediately starts crawling up the slope of the cockpit floor, slapping his hands down on the wood as if he cannot get there fast enough, his head raised almost straight up so that he looks like a turtle; but it makes Lucy anxious. Also, I am aware that this puts a strain on the Scatt, and as it is, Taylor has to pump every ten minutes or so. I try to keep us straight before the wind.

There are black clouds following us and night comes on ahead of time. By eight o'clock it is so dark that the cabin light penetrates only as far as our faces, and we have to keep the door shut and rely on our night vision. Instead of rising, as I thought it might, the wind has gone down to about fifteen knots, for which I am just as glad, as Taylor is no longer able to manage the pump. He lies groaning and miserable on his bunk, out of commission in sea-sickness-death. Fortunately, Paul is asleep and Lucy and I can take turns.

We are trying to sort out the lights ahead of us. For a long time they have all looked alike—streetlights, cars, buoys and the lights of houses. Finally, Lucy spots the three-second flashes of what should be the markers off the Point Judith breakwater, and I change course a little, hoping we are right. Suddenly, our stern is aflame. I crane my neck around to see a wake that for twenty or thirty yards behind us seems to be a pit of embers as wide as the boat and a good six feet deep. We have sailed into a sea of phosphorous; it is so bright it literally lights us on our way. We shoot through the black waters like a falling star, the Haley's comet of sailboats. Together we peer down into this sea of light, surprised by joy—quiet and timorous, like birds during a full eclipse of the sun. Ahead, as if in a dream, I see the jagged line of the breakwater. We sail into Point Judith at about nine-thirty, trailing clouds of glory, and anchor in the protected inner harbor as the rain begins to fall.

9

A Mind of Her Own

By eleven o'clock the next morning, we have all had enough of sitting in a cold, wet cabin, surrounded by miniature rain barrels; and we row ashore to drip-dry at a harbor side restaurant. The gale that came with the rain is still blowing, but here it is placid enough. The tiny harbor is packed with other boats, each one swinging in a different direction. We had a lot of trouble just finding a place to anchor. The forty-foot motor cruiser next to us had been particularly concerned lest we graze the ivory of her sides with our blue hull, and has piped me out on deck several times already this morning to discuss the possibility. I think of moving, but there is no place else to go; so, finally, I pull in a few feet of anchor line and let it go at that. I see him through the porthole doing sentry duty behind the plastic windows of his cockpit cover, but he appears to be satisfied, for he has not used his megaphone on me again. Now, as we row past the stern of his boat—Bree-Zee from Mamaroneck—I see that he, too, has gone ashore. High tide is at noon, and we are all hoping that the radio is right and that the storm will blow through in the early afternoon.

The windows of the small restaurant are fogged up and there is the atmosphere of a tepid sauna bath about the place. We add our gift of dripping slickers and stretched-out, soggy sweaters to the bulging coat racks and squash down at one of the tables. I disengage a discolored cigarette from the pack with swollen, leprous fingers and light up, affecting a casual, service-if-you-please nonchalance, and study the other occupants while we wait to order. The owner of ivory hull and a blowzy, middle-aged woman I take to be his wife are at the next table, and I grimace a how-do-you-do, pleased-to-meet-you, yes-it-certainly-is-rotten-weather to them and turn my attention to the menu. We order fish chowder and coffee all around. Lucy takes off another sweater and lets it plop to the floor. I want to remove my boots and try to restore my dishpanned feet, but I don't quite dare, sitting so near a man who looks like the judge of a circuit court. I have peeled down to my shirt and cannot go any further in that direction.

"What an adorable baby! I could have sworn when you came in that was Susan. Susan's our granddaughter. One of our granddaughters, I should say. She's Henry's second. Then there's..." Mrs. Bree-Zee, gone all gaga with grandmaternality. Lucy explains that Paul is a boy and that he won't be one year old until the 24th, and the old doll is so excited that she practically pulls their table over to join ours so she can talk without straining her voice. Fred, that's her husband, is fifty-seven, plays golf, recovered from a heart attack last year but was just made vice president of some can company, the name of which I didn't quite catch. They've been living in Mamaroneck, which they adore... She is pulling their table over to ours.

Fred has maintained a tomb-like silence, but as he rises to help with the furniture, he sees something out the window that makes him look as if he's about to suffer his second attack, and he belts out, "Your boat! Look at your boat. It's heading...I told you...anchor..."

But I am outside now, swimming as fast as I can toward the Scatt, which is sailing along at a good clip in the general direction of about a quarter million dollars' worth of cruising boats.

After an absurd ten or twelve strokes, I realize I'm not going to get anywhere; and I turn back to shore, throw off my boots and jump into the dinghy. At least she has missed Bree-Zee, I see as I row out into the current. The Scatt is halfway past a string of fancy yachts and headed for the far end of the harbor about a hundred yards away. Desperately, I pull on the oars, imagining years of servitude at some desk to pay for the Scatt's mayhemistic romp. Lucy and Taylor are running along just ahead of me. I arrive in time to see Fred step on board the Scatt and fasten her bowline to a piling on the dock. There is not even a scratch on her. She has dodged the entire fleet and moored herself in a place where the currents will not affect her. Where she can be more comfortable, and where no anchor can drag.

I fasten her stern line—there is no need for a bumper—and let Fred do all the head shaking on the way back. He's never seen anything like it in all his days. We certainly are lucky...

About one o'clock the wind subsides and the rain stops, and we spend a pleasant afternoon coasting down the swells toward the Cape Cod Canal.

10

Feasting

The next five days were a smorgasbord of delights. The water was ten degrees colder on the other side of the canal and sparkled like Vichy. The wind shifted conveniently to the SE and brought us the freshness of the open sea. There were interesting excursions into history. The difficulties our forefathers must have had trying to find a place to land in Plymouth Harbor were dramatized for us in a morning's protracted contemplation of a world of mud. No wonder they celebrated the Rock. There was fog off Boston harbor and we felt the ghostly presence of passing galleons. A tanker found us searching for the channel, but we did not insist on our right of way and followed him to safety instead. In Boston there were ship chandlers, and sea food, and the pleasure of entertaining a bug-eyed friend from Cambridge with champagne cocktails in the main cabin. Our yachting caps were stained by grime and sea water, and we wore them casually now and admired ourselves in the eyes of passing landlubbers. Long after we had lost our sea legs, we swaggered up through the cobblestone streets, conversing in French accents about fabulous voyages for the benefit of passersby.

Three days of this, a morning spent in the historical present of Gloucester, and then we were cricking through the narrow waterways that avoided Cape Ann, and patronizing the magnificence of the merely landed estates.

"What's the name of your ship and where are you from?"

"The Scatt II, Mantoloking, New Jersey."

"Bound?"

"Hancock Point, Maine."

"A good voyage!"

"A good day to you!"

The old man who took twenty minutes to get the drawbridge open for us seemed to delight as much as we did in holding up all those cars, in reminding the general public of the superior rights of sailing ships. A touch of New Hampshire, and then we were in Maine: Kittery, York, Kennebunkport, Old Orchard Beach and, finally, Portland Light and the thirty-mile open stretch of Casco Bay.

"I know what we said, but if we sail way in there it'll take at least two days to get across." I was pushing for a straight run to Cape Small. We'd be fifteen miles offshore most of the way, but that seemed nothing to me now with so many leagues behind us. The Scatt had been maligned, I felt. Look how well she had done off Point Judith. If she leaked a bit more in a heavy wind, that just meant a little extra work at the pump. We could really sail anywhere in her. The truth was that after almost two weeks, I was dying to get to the real sailing country, to the island-studded passages of Muscongus and Penobscot bays. In my family's nineteen-foot sloop, I had been as far west as North Haven, and once, foolhardily, forty miles east to Roque Island. Casco Bay had lots of islands too, but we could explore them some other time.

There was a dead calm the morning we motored out of Portland Harbor, Lucy and I still arguing about which way to go. Taylor was on my side, though not for the same reasons. Conrad and Melville must have had stronger stomachs than he did, he told us. A calm day was to be taken advantage of to get as far as you could. He himself, when he became rich, would invest in a motor launch and spend much of his time in port. Or perhaps he would just drive around in his chauffeured limousine, wearing his yachting cap. He wasn't saying he was anxious for the trip to be over, it was just that...

The signs were auspicious, I kept telling Lucy. What's more, we'd had the motor checked over in Boston and hadn't had to look at it since. We'd be in Boothbay by evening if we went straight. We could just omit this little change in plans when we next spoke to Mama Reeves.

Eventually, I won out and we headed off into a haze that veiled the further shores of Casco Bay from our eyes and allowed us the excitement of imagining we were headed straight out to sea.

11

Night Lights

We were about a third of the way across when the wind hit. High cirrus clouds raced toward us out of the NE. The slate gray of the sea cracked into vivid blues and whites; and we began to prance to the east, each dip of the bow salting us down with fine spray. It was the first time we had sailed close-hauled into a good wind. With her sail in like this, the end of her thirty-foot boom seemingly bounced on the waves, with green water scouring her deck as the wind freshened still more. It was as if the matronly Scatt had become eighteen again—a girl in a summer dress running across a clover-studded field, an Atalanta who had no need of golden spheres to elude the grasping arms, who could go on, untiring, like this forever.

We all felt it, even Taylor, this sense of having reached the top, as if Maine were the other side of a hill we had been climbing for too long and the days before us were going to be a shushing descent through fields of powder, dotted here and there with islands of spruce. The wind in your face, rather than at your neck; that was part of it. Your nostrils flared of their own accord. You sat up straighter and sucked in great lungfuls of sea air, as if what you had been breathing before had already been used by someone else. The world had been old and now was new again. Your eyes, too. Between the showers of spray, beneath their salt-encrusted brows, your eyes saw further and more sharply: diamond-sight, jeweled motion, jewels amid jewels. The whole bay was visible now: the islands way off to our left that looked to be the shore itself, the hills beyond them, the low silhouette of Cape Small in front of us, the cloud shadows that dappled everything with ever-changing patterns of light and color. It was as if we had sailed into a kaleidoscope. We danced there at its center—breaking, reforming ourselves, breaking again; both the pattern and the eye that looked, ecstatic; wishing for nothing else than that the dance could go on forever.

It was Taylor who noticed it, the noise of something banging at the closed cabin doors. He looked in. One of our suitcases was floating there in more than a foot of water.

"What's happened?" said Lucy.

"She's opened up on us," I said. Now that it had happened, the expression seemed particularly vivid. The planks on the hull were wrenched apart by that wrecking bar of a mast, the sea dribbled through at first and then gushed in where it found a break in the caulking, the cracks widened, the fastenings turned in the rotted wood—old wounds opening. Frailty, youth, arrows, death.

"What should we do?" Lucy said, her face white.

"I don't know," I answered, momentarily obsessed by the vision of something human but also animal painfully dying beneath me; me unable to help, participating in the act even, guilty, hating the killer. It was as if the girl had turned her teasing eyes back to me for a second and so missed seeing the hole, had been thrown forward, her forehead striking a rock, had broken both her legs and was looking up through the bloody mat of her hair for me to tell her that nothing had happened— that instant before the pain begins, that time lapse when one tries to unsee what it is that has happened, and cannot, and then the pain comes, the face torn and made inhuman by it before it goes blank, all but the terrified eyes.

I opened the hatch to look at the engine. Too late. It was more than half underwater and useless to us now. I knew, vaguely, what we should do, but it somehow never occurred to me that we would do it. We should get the sail down, throw out a pail or something on the end of a rope as a sea anchor to keep the bow up into the wind, and let ourselves be blown out to sea. Without that pressure of the mast forcing her planks apart, they would close up again and we could pump her out and wait for the wind to die, or shift. Eventually, (if we didn't sink, or break up under the force of a still greater wind—though already it might be too late. A plank might have been pried loose, several planks. The gashing wounds in her hull might not close...), eventually, someone would come to our aid.

The trouble was that this was no storm at all, just a good wind—fifteen or twenty knots. How could we lower sail and act as if these were rescue conditions? There were two other sailboats a mile or so off. They had been behind us when the wind started, but were ahead now; big sloops, our size or a little larger. They were heeled way over—racing.

Taylor had the pump out, but the Scatt was rolling so that he could not get his balance. "Bail it straight out into the cockpit," I yelled at him. "Lucy, get another bucket and help him." If we could stay on this course, and if they could keep even with the water, we would be all right. Maybe I was wrong. Maybe the leak wasn't a bad one. It was over an hour since Taylor last pumped. Maybe something was open. "Check the head. It might be coming in there. That pipe under the sink, too." There was no way of knowing about the other through-hull fittings. The rubber hoses that drained the water from the cockpit down through the bottom of the boat disappeared into the ocean of the bilge. If they had broken off, they would flail around like eels, wouldn't they?

"Nothing's coming in there," said Taylor, sloshing back through the water. Luckily, Paul was asleep. At this slant, the raised side of the engine hatch made a perfect spot for him, out of the wind and high and dry. He had been sleeping on this perch, wrapped in a blanket, for the past half hour.

The Scatt was heavy with water, though, and every so often a larger wave would come along and the tip of the boom would be caught in its breaking crest, giant fingers of foam would rush up past the line of reef points toward the hovering gaff and we would practically come to a halt, swerve downwind and only at the last minute, it seemed, come bucking out of it and start off again. Had the wind been really strong, we would have capsized, certainly, dead in the water like that. As it happened, though, the boom would rise out of the sea, like a whale breaching, as soon as the body of the wave passed under it, and the water would cascade from the belly of the sail and we would be off again. It slowed us down, and took us off course, which was the real danger, for we were just barely able to head up as far as Cape Small.

I discovered that if I let the sail out just as I saw the crest of the wave rising toward it, the tip of the boom would fly out into the trough where the wave could not reach it. In order to keep us on course, though, I would then have to pull the sail back in instantly. This would have been no problem on my parents' sloop, but on the Scatt it was a different matter. A hundred, two hundred pounds of pressure? It was more than I could handle even with both my arms, and I needed one hand for steering. But I could sit on the high side, on the bench above and to the right of where Paul was peacefully sleeping, steer with my right foot, brace my left on the engine hatch and with the mainsheet held around my shoulders, I could bend down toward the hatch so that I was crouching, standing really, on my left leg. The boom would swing out of danger and then I would push off with my left leg until I was leaning way back on the seat and the sail was in again where it should be. It was not really much harder than doing deep knee bends or rowing in a heavy sea. It was a juggling act, something of a gamble, too, as I tried to judge the wave's size, the length of its leap, correctly.

It took all my energy, all my concentration, to row like this, to slide down and then up this invisible ramp, though after a time I did not think about it. I was the boom. The strands of rope that connected us disappeared. I felt the pull of the sail on me, the weight of the gaff, the tension on each mast hoop; the pressure, the wrenching pressure of the mast itself, the very fibers of the wood stretching like tiny muscles; the tension in the stays; in the bolts that ran through the hull plates that held the stays down, and in the jutting iron arms of the crosstrees.

Every once in a while, though, I would be thrown. My foot would slip on the wet varnish of the wheel. The mainsheet would scream out through the blocks, and I would have to stand up and pull in the sail with both hands as the Scatt headed herself up into the wind, lost headway and then came plunging back. Or a monstrous wave would catch the tip of the boom in spite of me, and I would be pitched over the motor hatch; I would have been thrown into the sea if I hadn't let go of the sheet in time. The Scatt would be dead in the water now, would tilt another ten degrees, and I would know that it could not tip any more without going over, would watch the water foaming into the cockpit, and would wait, simply wait to see what was going to happen. And then, with a shudder, the sea would slip by the outstretched arm of the boom, and the Scatt would break ahead, and I would be trying to get the mainsheet in again as fast as I could so as not to slip too far downwind. Each time this happened, Lucy and Taylor would stop their bailing and look over at me and the three of us would hold our strained positions while the Scatt balanced there on the brink of the void.

The wind had started about noon. It was getting dark when we spotted the reef far ahead of us and just to our right. The waves seemed to be breaking right over it, though from the chart that didn't seem possible. Just beyond it was Cape Small, but we had to sail past the reef to get there.

For the past three hours we had made little headway. Though Lucy and Taylor had been bailing steadily, the water had been slowly gaining on them. It was almost up to their knees and within a few inches of the cockpit floor. We were heavy in the sea and the tide was against us.

We did not really make a decision. It just happened. I doubt that Taylor and Lucy even knew that there were choices that could be made. They had left that to me long ago. And I, I felt like part of a process that was simply working itself out and no more free to act outside of the chain of events that had led up to the present moment than was the boom, or the sail, or the mast, or any other part of the boat; or the sea, or the wind, for that matter. There was a part of me also that was detached from our condition that had nothing to do with fear or anxiety or hope or even strength, a part of me that was united with the Scatt, but not just with her: with the wind and the sea and the rocks ahead and the blood red sky and the vastness of the elemental earth and the heavens; a part of me that I had no idea even existed but that had been slowly blossoming in the last few hours. While I got weaker, more tired, clumsier, while I degenerated into a mindless automaton, my secret self grew in strength. It delighted in prying those planks away from the rotten wood. Its heartbeat quickened when the wind gusted to twenty-five knots, or when a ten-foot comber buried the boom and dashed its green side fifteen feet up the sail. It would laugh aloud in high merriment if we capsized, or if the mast suddenly cracked and came crashing down into the sea or on top of our heads. Yet it gloried, too, this secret self, in the afterlight of the sunset, in the reddened foam of the waves. It looked to the west and picked out Venus when the skies darkened, and it greeted her as an equal, triumphantly.

For a long time now, I had had Paul tucked into my shirt. There was no other safe, dry place for him.

Lucy had managed to feed him something, though the rest of us had had nothing but a few crackers since breakfast, and for several hours he had been hanging, papoose style, just below my chin, held under his arms by the "V" of my flannel shirt. Now he was sleeping again. We warmed each other, his sense of security making me, too, feel protected.

We were floundering along just inside the reef by this time, close enough to hear loose boulders being pulled along the bottom with the suction of the retreating waves, near enough to see the seaweed-skirted menace of a jutting rock rise out of the waves in front of us as we lost our steerage. The surf was roaring. "Roaring," the best and most literal word for it—the noise the lion tamer must steel himself to and then encourage for the benefit of the delicious fears of those who sit in the stands excitedly crunching peanuts: the deafening sound of hundreds, of thousands of lions trapped by seven-foot Watusis at the end of a blind canyon; the maddened cacophonies Daniel must have heard before he heard another voice that calmed the lions' fears. I knew where we were by the steady sound of breaking surf, but we were barely moving past it. We were numbed, though, now, past fear or any emotion, past awareness of time even, alive only in our ears and arms and backs.

My secret self, though, was in rapture. The whole sky before us was aflame with northern lights. The stars themselves were all but fused as one shimmering blaze after another shook the sky. Northern lights, the searchlights of the gods: Odin, Thor, Valhalla, the ride of the Valkyries. Yet softer, like a veil of silent lightning lifting and falling in the breeze. The sky was dancing. It was as if each star had suddenly been freed from its course and granted infinite speed—a break, a holiday from the everlasting pattern—to glorify creation itself. They rose, and burst, and split asunder, and fell apart and reformed themselves. Or one would glide in a perfect arc across the sky, and another, and still another, would intersect its path and not come within light years of it, and then the whole sky would melt and dissolve itself into a fountain of light. Yet there was a pattern, a pulse, that seemed to govern all. Brighter. Dimmer. Here. Now over there. A flicker across the top. An answering ripple above the dark line of the earth. As the dance ended, I felt my secret self edge away a little. I could not hold it, and then it was gone, and gradually I became aware of the other light.

I had been steering by it for several hours now, I realized. It was steady and had been getting brighter. Except for the stars, it was the only light there was.

The roar of the breakers had diminished. We must be past the reef, out of danger, nearing the protection of the Cape. And as I thought this, the wind just stopped, as suddenly as if a hand had flicked it off, and we rolled mildly in a sea that was practically calm. We could see the dim shoreline ahead of us and to our left. The light shone like a tiny moon. We let down the sail and anchored in about thirty feet of water. "Let out all the line," I said to Taylor. "In case the wind comes up." I lit the riding light and got my first good look into the cabin. It was filled. We were awash. The water was at least a foot deep in the cockpit, not more than three feet from the ceiling of the cabin. The self-bailing drains had had to be plugged hours ago. We floated only a few inches above the water, like a great sunken whale. But we floated. The Scatt would not sink, could not, had enough natural buoyancy to float the lead on her keel, that massive engine, other bits of deadweight, and us. I felt suddenly light-hearted, yet at the next moment I trembled at the thought that she might have sunk on us out there. The possibility had never occurred to me until now.

There was almost no freeboard at all in the little dinghy, and Taylor had to bail steadily with a can while Lucy held Paul and we tried not to move. I rowed slowly toward the light. There were breakers in front of us now but they sounded like small pebbles moving, a chunking noise followed by a soft swish. On our right we could make out the dim shapes of rocks. There was a bit of a swell, but it was gentle. How big was the surf? Might there be an undertow? If we went over I would take Paul, I said. We couldn't be very far away from shore. Try to hold on to the boat as long as possible. Surely we couldn't get this close to safety and not make it. I rowed on, gingerly, wanting to get us in far enough so that we wouldn't have to swim.

"You're getting close," Lucy said. And then we were out of the dinghy, and I was holding Paul up above my head. I saw the dinghy riding bottom up toward shore, and Lucy and Taylor walking in behind it. We staggered through one last wave and then we were safe on the beach, and Taylor had hold of the boat and he and I were dragging it up on the sand until finally we could drop it and tie the line to a railing attached to some old wooden stairs.

The light was above us and then, suddenly, it went out. We slowly dragged ourselves up the stairs, clutching the railing for support, and I thought, "Shipwrecked! We've been shipwrecked!"

"My heavens. Whatever has happened to you? And you have a baby! Why, you're soaked to the skin. Come right in." And now a man was standing there, too, and behind him I could see a cozy-looking wood-paneled living room, the red coals of a fire in a stone hearth and then we were inside and sitting down, and already it all seemed like a dream.

They had been expecting guests. That was why the porch light was on. They had just given them up and were on their way to bed. They almost never stayed up past ten and here it was practically midnight. Wasn't it lucky, they both kept saying, bringing us bowls of steaming tomato soup. Theirs was the only house within miles, too. We could move right into the guest house. It was all made up. There was a spare room upstairs for Taylor. Mr. Hatfield got most of the story from us, but they had to piece it together from what each of us said, and it couldn't have made much sense. He called the Coast Guard. There was a station at the mouth of the Kennebec. They would try to locate the Scatt right away. They didn't think it advisable to leave it where it was all night. If the wind shifted... Fine, fine. Wonderful.

The Hatfields' winter home was in Englewood, New Jersey. Did they by any chance know the Whitings? Of course. Clint, Maggie? My grandparents. Their neighbors. It was too much, too much to be believed.

12

The Morning After

Through the plate glass, the morning, as if newly made, advanced to meet me. The little bay where we had landed, the line of reefs and the open, white-flecked sea beyond was a scene as familiar and inviting as the one from the bedroom of the house in Hancock Point. Without moving from the bed, I could reach out and with my fingers trace the grains of pine on the bureau across the room, so near it seemed, so sharply etched, in the sparkling clarity. The faint, delicious tang of wood smoke was like the bacon smell of breakfast. We woke almost together and in seconds we were outside, standing on the slight rise behind the main house, laughing, looking with wonder at every detail as if we'd been asleep for twenty years, as if we were children who had found themselves in a garden of peacock tails. Even after it began to come back—the memory of darkness and of night—there was still this coltish excitement inside of us, this certainty that nothing but marvels could greet us on such a day.

We couldn't look properly surprised, just kept nodding our heads and smiling idiotically when Mr. Hatfield told us that the Scatt was bailed out and ready for us at the Coast Guard Station about a mile away. Of course. As it should be. After breakfast, we all drove around to see her and hear the story.

With the Scatt nestled there in front of us up against the dock, it was hard to take in the details. As we drove in, there was a sailor perched on the crosstrees untangling a lobster trap from the rigging. A lobster trap? An older man called out from below, "Anything in it?"

"Two keepers and a short."

"Bring it on down."

Chief Steward strolled over to us. "We cut loose the others—oh, maybe eight of them," he said, pointing to a tangle of ropes on the dock. "But that one, it was snubbed tight right up at the top. I thought she was towing hard, but I hadn't figured she'd made a clean sweep of the bay."

"You mean she tipped over on you?" I said, our eyes following the descent of the trap down the mast.

"We'd put Harvard aboard to steer her and there he was at the end of his line, floundering around in the water, so we fell back and picked him up..."

"Then what happened?" I said.

"I was going to cut her loose, but Dave said, 'Let me try her' and he turned the wheel down and gunned her until I thought we were going to go over ourselves, and then he brought her up again and gunned her some more, and, by gorry, up she popped—lobster traps swinging from her mast, and that one there perched right on top. Isn't a hell of a lot showing, I'll tell you, when she turns turtle like that. Anyway, we got her here about daybreak."

The boys had joined us by then and they were all three grinning, as if they'd just gotten back from a fire and it turned out to be nothing but smoke from a squirrel's nest in the chimney.

"Harvard Lounder and Dave Preble," said the Chief.

"Glad to meet you," I said, and we shook hands all around, everyone grinning foolishly.

Looking at the Scatt now, I could hardly believe she had tipped over, had almost dragged a man to his death, would have, if he had not had a life line tied to him. The mast wasn't even scratched. Could it really have been churning back and forth fifty feet under the sea and escaped splintering itself on the bottom? Surely the water was not that deep? It was thirty feet where we had anchored. Were they kidding us? Was that the explanation for all this strange joviality? Were they making us pay something, at any rate, for the sleepless night and the threat of danger? That lobster trap at the top of the mast—might they have made all that up? Hauled the trap up there themselves? Then I noticed the ribbon of kelp fluttering like some desperate flag from where it had jammed itself between the top of the forestay and the mast, and knew they would never have gone that far, and what the Chief had been saying began to take on shape and meaning.

What would we have done if she had capsized on us? We hadn't even thought of lifelines. Would we have had the presence of mind to grab something as the hull tipped up and then over us? Taylor and Lucy would have been trapped in the cabin, drowned or swept away into the night if they had managed to get out. Could I have avoided the hull's crashing weight above me, held on to Paul, grabbed a rope and then pulled us up onto the slippery bottom of the boat? Could I have stayed there any length of time in forty-eight degree water while ten-foot waves broke over us?

They'd pumped her out in a few hours, they said. Still leaked some, but not too much. She might look all right from here but wait till we looked inside. We climbed on board. For some reason what held my eyes the longest was the oatmeal plastered across the ceiling—like someone's brains. The rest of the cabin was such a mess that at first I couldn't distinguish details. Seaweed hung from the hooks where coffee cups had been, cans were without their labels and most of them were on the floor. A pot, caught by the rim of the bunk on which I slept, was half filled with water; all the mattresses were piled over on the far right covering Paul's "crib"; loose potatoes were everywhere, as were soggy heaps of clothing, ripped charts and a book lying face down in what looked like mud, and Paul's chair, with the potty missing and the lid broken off was jammed in on top of the ice box.

Taylor, who kept his clothes in a duffel, was neater than we were. At first we thought the duffel had gone overboard, but finally he found it wedged behind the toilet.

Lucy took a look and then sank down with a groan onto a bench in the cockpit, next to the Hatfields. Part of me, too, wanted to take the whole soggy mess and throw it overboard. It would take days to clean this up, hours just to find out what was missing. Stronger, though, was the sense of what we had escaped.

* * *

At three o'clock that afternoon we were at the boatyard in Bath. Harvard and Dave had towed us up there. They were going anyway, they said, to pick up some stuff. Might as well take us along. I had found a bottle of champagne and we gave it to them when we said goodbye, joking about how well it would go with those lobsters. We were to leave the Scatt here for the motor to be fixed and were expecting my parents to pick us up within the next hour.

Taylor was taking a three-thirty bus back to the city. He said he had plenty of material to write about now and that there was no need to push his luck any further. Besides, he wanted to show up at the bookstore before his calluses peeled off. With his scrubby brown beard and beaten-up yachting cap, he insisted that he now resembled the young Joseph Conrad and he wanted to get back to his apartment and his typewriter before the vision faded. Conrad a la Saki. He assured us it had never been done.

When the engine was fixed, Lucy would drive my father, my younger brother and me down here again, and the three of us would bring the Scatt the remaining seventy-five miles to Hancock Point. We would use the sail only if the wind was behind us. Otherwise, we would motor.

The Scatt had given us fair warning. Until we

could afford to supply her with new ribs and some solid planking to go around them, we were to be very easy on her. My vision of racing the phantoms of Indian war canoes through the island-studded bays to our east would have to wait.

PART TWO

THE TOURIST TRADE

1

The Idea Is Born

We were living in Florida at the time, where I was doing graduate work in English. If we had an extra dime, it went for a better brand of tuna fish. Supported, in part, by both Lucy's mother and my parents, we were hardly in a position to rebuild the Scatt. My mother's suggestion was that we drive the boat up onto the shore and make a children's playhouse out of her. My father, fingering the blisters on his pumping hand, was equally pessimistic. For a while we toyed with the idea of taking the Scatt out off Mount Desert when there was a good SE wind blowing, advertising the event well in advance to be assured of a large ticket-holding crowd, and then driving her head on into the frothing jaws of Thunder Hole, a self-inflicted giant destruct of a shipwreck that would thrill the souls of the multitude. We might even be able to interest a movie company in the event. I would become famous as a daredevil skipper. We'd end up by making a pile of money and then we could buy another boat, one that you could heel over in a light breeze without feeling you were suicidal.

How would we get me off the wreck, though? Invisible wires spun from the end of a giant crane perched on the forty-foot cliffs, just out of reach of the cameras; these would pull me to safety from the splintering deck just in the nick of time. Or perhaps I would climb to the crosstrees, somehow control the boat from there, and then, just before the mast snapped, casually step off onto the cliff to the cheers of thousands.

I suppose it was this notion of selling tickets that made us think of using the Scatt as a tourist boat. The idea blossomed at some time during the winter, and by

June, when we were more than ready to head for cooler climes, it had bloomed into a rich and exotic plan. By Labor Day we would be salting down the shekels.

The scheme was simple. All great ideas, once they are stated, strike us as obvious. Bar Harbor, seven miles across the bay from Hancock Point, was fast becoming the tourist mecca of the eastern seaboard. There were plenty of excursion boats to service the more mundane needs of the city dwellers, but nothing for the sailing enthusiast, not even small boats for hire; no comfortable, large sailing vessel on which ten to fifteen could loll and recapture the past. We needed only to advertise our presence.

Every day for two weeks we drove to the boatyard in Sorrento, ten miles away, where we had berthed the Scatt for the winter, and this time we spent our energies caulking and puttying, and refastening below the waterline. At lunch time, in the car and during the evenings, Lucy would examine me on the Rules of the Road. When I thought I was ready, I would drive to Portland, astound the local official with my brilliance and return home a captain, fully licensed to carry passengers for hire on vessels under forty tons on the inland waterways of the United States, including the Great Lakes and the coastal waters within the territorial limits of same. I wasn't trying to get into the Merchant Marine. Three miles out was enough for me.

We had a plate made from a photograph of the Scatt taken from the dinghy that showed several people standing around on the deck while others sunbathed on the cabintop. This was the eye-catcher for the posters and flyers we had made. With her gaff-rigged sail set way out to starboard, not only did the Scatt look like a coastal schooner at least twice her size, but even more to the point, the picture seemed to justify the words that were printed in bold-faced type beneath it. Posters and flyers read the same, as follows:

We purchased the largest megaphone we could find—three feet long and made out of durable cardboard—and Lucy painted Scatt II in bold, blue lettering on opposite sides of it. This we would use to drum up trade on the streets of Bar Harbor. We made a three-by-five-foot billboard out of wood and cardboard on which Scatt II again appeared in blue lettering, against a white field this time, to make it more impressive, and underneath it an arrow. We would attach this to the rigging while in port. We considered painting "Sail on the Scatt II" in six-foot letters across the sail for the benefit of prospective passengers on shore, but finally dismissed this idea as too crassly commercial.

The idea was that I would sail over to Bar Harbor and back again each day. What I needed to find now was someone to sail with me, more precisely, a first mate, someone to man the pump, for in spite of our labors, the Scatt leaked somewhat more than she had the summer before. Even if she had wanted to, Lucy was too busy with the family now to help me. Over the winter we had grown to five: there was Patrick, born in March, and Tessa, aged eleven, Lucy's niece, whom we had adopted.

That seemed to be the only remaining problem, finding a boy with a strong right arm who didn't mind being maligned by me to the group aboard in order to hide the true nature of his activities. The Scatt still leaked. Yes. But if someone were on hand at the pump on a full-time basis, there was no real danger in that. The concept would be difficult to explain, however. The plan we worked out was that my assistant would retire to the cabin shortly after we pushed off from the dock, shut the doors, turn on a battery-powered radio and remain there until the trip was over. When asked what he was doing below all the time when he might be on deck assisting me, I would shake my head and sadly explain that this comic book and radio addict was all that I had been able to get in the way of crew. Meanwhile, of course, the boy would be pumping like a madman, the disturbing sloshings of the water hidden by the music from the radio.

It took the right kind of lad to fit into such a scheme and also to accept a commission instead of a straight salary. Twenty percent of the take was what I had in mind. I asked around the boatyard and finally he appeared: a tall, thin, lazy-looking red-headed kid of seventeen named Bobby, who proved not only to be strong, willing and able, but to possess a poker-faced wit as well. The only aspect of the plan he balked at was the idea of megaphoning through the streets of Bar Harbor scaring up the trade. Besides being distasteful to him, he quite rightly pointed out that such aggressiveness was out of keeping with his role as a no-good. If I was to be the front man, let me do the barking as well. Okay. The deal was made. It was the 25th of June and all that now remained were a few technicalities: my captain's license and a successful Coast Guard inspection of the

Scatt. I felt well-prepared for the exam and was driving to Portland in the morning. As far as the Coast Guard approval went, I had been told that it was virtually automatic as long as you had the proper number of life preservers, fire extinguishers, and such aboard.

2

A Trip to Portland

"How far astern do you tow a seventy-five foot barge?"

I took a wild guess, and he told me to come back in three weeks. Three weeks! It was only a few days until the end of June, and already the tourists were piling into Bar Harbor. I had to get started or I couldn't hope to cash in on the crop. Also, I'd arranged to be inspected by the Coast Guard the next morning. What would they think...?

I sank down into a straight-backed chair in the gloomy dungeon of my inquisitor's office and looked across at him in disbelief. I wasn't going to tow barges. Why didn't he ask me about riding lights or right of ways? Couldn't I please come back this afternoon and try again? From Hancock Point to Portland was a five-hour drive. It was eleven o'clock. If I studied hard, I was sure I could do better next time. I hadn't realized that I was supposed to memorize everything in the book. There were one or two places I had skipped; I admitted that. If I just had a few more hours... Please?

A longish wait. I pictured him standing on the bridge, weighing the decision in his mind. I begged him with a craven look in my eyes. I tried to look humble, yet worthy. Finally, the granite face of this retired sea captain softened sufficiently to allow the words to escape: "Three-thirty sharp. Office shuts at four." And I left. Where to go? There was a park across the street and I found myself a bench and started to memorize my way through the fifty-page pamphlet, the thought of a diet that did not include even tuna fish during the coming year spurring me on to Herculean efforts. The sun passed over my head unobserved as I sat there cramming all kinds of useless information into my head: the tensile strength of all the possible sizes of manila rope, and the proper lighting of barges and channel markings and other buoys in the Mississippi River. And, of course, the prescribed distance at which to tow a seventy-five foot barge.

My bench harbored others besides myself during those four hours, but as far as I was concerned, the port was fog bound. I was vaguely aware of their presence, but only one of them did I see, an elderly woman whose "Well! Of all the uncivil people..." penetrated the steel hull of my mind and rocked me into a consciousness of her existence when she steamed off to a more friendly anchorage.

I was terrified that either I would not finish the book in time, or that, having gotten to the last page, I would discover that I'd missed the appointment. So I sat there, watch in hand, timing my own mental wind sprints as I tried to soak up the pages.

It was three-twenty. I had not eaten and had had to skim the last five pages, fascinating as they were. I was running back across the street and climbing the stairs three at a time lest I arrive a second late and have the door slammed in my face. And then I was in the dungeon once again, and the old sea captain cracked open his mouth and said, "How far astern do you tow a seventy-five foot barge?"

And I replied, "When she's full or empty, sir?"
And he growled, "When she's full."
I told him and he gave me my license.

3

The Big Day

"Scatt's in."

"How is she?"

"Not much."

Two boys on the pier at Bar Harbor. Lucy reported the exchange to me later in the day. We'd had trouble with the engine and, as there was practically no wind, we didn't get into Bar Harbor until ten-thirty. A bad way to begin, disappointing all those tourists, I thought, as I walked up the ramp and over to the Tourist Information Center. My stride was purposeful. I was a man of business. There were a lot of people milling about, munching on ice cream cones, but I looked to neither left nor right. Later on I would play the huckster with my three-foot megaphone, but at the moment I was Captain Trowbridge, reporting in late, ready to take on cargo.

The place was packed. One of the girls was working out the trails on a map of Acadia National Park for a man in lederhosen who had a baby strapped in a sort of knapsack thing on his back. His wife was glancing over the clutter of leaflets spread out on a long table against the wall. I resisted the impulse to shove one of mine into her hands. The two other girls were trying to get motel accommodations for a tired-looking, middle-aged foursome. When the mountaineering couple was finished, I sidled up to Kathie and, trying to keep the dollar signs from registering, said, "Anyone been in for the Scatt this morning?"

"Oh, Captain Trowbridge. If you'd only been here yesterday. There was a party of ten. They were dying to go out with you... I tried to get them to wait over another day, but they couldn't."

"Thanks. What about this morning? Was there anyone here earlier? I came in a little late, you know."

"No. No one's been in today. Not yet. There's not much wind, is there? Yesterday was perfect. Gee, I'm sorry you missed those people. They were talking about the afternoon sail and the lobster picnic, too."

Good old Kathie. I'd definitely have to take her and the other girls out for a free trip. Eighty dollars. Minus the lobsters and stuff. Call it seventy dollars. Oh, well. Maybe there were some people at the boat now. I smiled at the harbor master, who was sitting in his tiny office smoking a pipe and staring out the window, and walked back to the boat, trying to dismiss the lost cargo from my mind. Bobby had put the sign up. It looked great. Now if I was a tourist in Bar Harbor and I saw that sign...

Bobby was below, stretched out on one of the bunks. He'd just finished pumping. No, no one had been around. I hadn't been kidding about how she leaked? No, I guess probably not. Where was the megaphone? I didn't mention the ten people who'd been here the day before.

Actually, yesterday, the 30th, was to have been our fourth day, but the Coast Guard had held us up. They said we needed a flame arrester for the carburetor. I wasn't even sure where the carburetor was, and now, finally, after waiting three days for it, now that it was on and we were allowed to operate, the crummy engine didn't work anyway. I tried to calm down, think of the bright side. They'd passed us, hadn't they? Secondhand life preservers and everything. And no embarrassing questions about the condition of the vessel.

I turned on my circus voice—loud and clear. "Sail on the Scatt II. Afternoon sail leaves at one o'clock from the municipal pier. Three dollars for adults. A dollar-fifty for children under twelve. Get your tickets now and avoid the rush." I was walking up the hill toward the center of town barking through the megaphone and feeling like a total idiot. Half an hour later, hoarse and sweating like a pig, I was on my way back to the boat, having already developed strong negative feelings about my potential clientele.

"I neva' hoid of a scattoo, did you, Al?"

"Put it on your head, fella. That's where it belongs."

I thought of cramming the cardboard megaphone into the litter barrel in front of the Dairy Queen. Carrying it was like walking through town and pretending you have clothes on when actually you knew you were naked. I'd had dreams like that, but somehow in the dreams you got away with it. I was walking fast now, holding the megaphone at my side by the mouthpiece, trying to pretend it wasn't really connected with me, when a car tooted and I looked up and it was Lucy and the kids. I crammed the megaphone in ahead of me and sank blissfully into the seat next to Lucy.

We drove down to where the Scatt was tied up and Bobby said a man and his wife and kid had signed up for the afternoon sail. They were off getting something to eat. He pulled seven singles and a fifty-cent piece out of his pocket and handed it over. Our first dough. Ceremoniously, I peeled off a dollar and handed him that and the change. Lucy took three dollars. The car needed gas. I put the other three dollars in my pocket.

We were in business.

4

The Spivaks

None of the Spivaks had ever been sailing before. The boy stood next to his mother, clinging to her arm while she sat poker-straight in the only comfortable chair in the cockpit. Her husband, on the seat next to her, was an old-looking middle-aged man with a lined, sallow face, thin, sandy hair and large bony hands.

There was a very light SE wind and we were drifting past the lee side of Bald Porcupine, a little too close, so that what wind there was had been taken by the sheer fifty-foot cliffs. We'd learned only that they lived in Bayonne, New Jersey, and were here on their week's vacation, and then Lucy also lapsed into silence. Two and a half more hours of this, I thought—and then I saw the eagle.

Actually, I heard him. And the boy must have heard him at the same instant, for he jumped up onto the motor hatch. It was a bald eagle with what looked like a good six-foot wingspan circling above the cliffs and making shrill, cat-like cries, as if we'd gotten too close to his nest and he was trying to chase us away.

Mrs. Spivak, her voice strangely soft and musical, said, "He's seen his first one. Now he'll see more."

As it happened, their son, Mark, at the age of eight, was an expert on birds. Living in Bayonne, he hadn't seen very many in the flesh, not outside of zoos, anyway. And a bald eagle! Well, it was rare enough to find one of those up here.

Paul and Patrick were both below, lulled into instant naps by the motion of the boat. The wind had caught us now, and Tessa had gone up by the mast. Then she sat down and, holding on to the stays, leaned way out so that with one foot she could touch the bow wave. Mark followed after her before his parents could stop him. And then they were both reaching down toward the foam with their legs, shrieking in unison when a wave soaked their feet and looking back at us each time it did, the way kids do on a merry-go-round.

Mr. Spivak took a camera out of his wife's purse and snapped a picture of them, and after a little persuasion he got her to come up next to him on the cabintop. For the next half hour, until we reached the tip of Ironbound Island, the two of them sat there, rocking gently back and forth and gazing out past the only visible land between here and Portugal: Egg Rock, its lighthouse tiny from this distance, sky and sea melting into one another.

Two blue herons flew out from among the dead trees above the cliffs on the sea side of Ironbound, and I told the Spivaks about the rookery—thirty or forty nests the last time we'd been there—and the primeval-looking forest of giant spruces you came to just before you got there. I almost wished I hadn't mentioned it, they looked so disappointed when I said there was not time to stop now. But then Lucy said, "You could take them tomorrow, couldn't you, Clint? Drop them off in the morning and pick them up again during the afternoon sail?"

"Sure," I said, and their faces lit up and it was arranged.

We were about a mile from Bar Harbor when the wind died. It was three-thirty and we were drifting out with the falling tide toward Bald Porcupine and the sea. I made a show of starting the engine, but of course it didn't work. I was about to turn the wheel over to Lucy and start towing us with the rowboat when Mr. Spivak asked me if I had a tool box. I knew from his manner that this was his territory. I had developed a completely fatalistic attitude toward engines and this one in particular, but they seemed to make his eyes shine with love. The starter was frozen, he said. If I had such and such a wrench and some oil, he would try to free it. I got him the tool box and in no time he had the starter gripped in his left hand and was twisting at the top of it as if what he was holding were a refractory jar of peanut butter or something; and then, with a grunt of satisfaction, the veins in his forearm swollen to the size of pencils, he broke the parts free.

Five minutes later the motor was running and I had had my first real lesson in mechanics. If she made that whirring noise again, just a tap of the hammer—here—would engage the starter. The engine sounded pretty good otherwise, but tomorrow he would bring his own tool box, check the points and set the gaps on the plugs. I tried to pay him when we left each other at the dock, but he wouldn't hear of it. We waved goodbye, till the morning, through the fine drizzle that had started to fall, and Bobby and I started back toward Hancock Point.

No more business for today. Rained out. Then why did I feel so elated? Was it because Mr. Spivak had gotten the motor running? Partly. But that didn't seem to account for this expansiveness I felt—as if I had just been made a trustee of the Ford Foundation or something and was a benevolent distributor of infinite largesse. It was the eagle, I decided, and the herons, and the motion of the boat with the kids riding on the bow, and the bay itself, with all its islands, that I had sailed in ever since I could remember, but for the first time now in my own boat. But mainly, it was the Spivaks.

5

Bobby

There were eight other people at the dock the next morning besides the Spivaks, two of them thanks to our friends' enthusiasm at the restaurant the night before. Could we sail past the eagle's nest? Would we see herons?

While we were talking, Mr. Spivak tuned up the motor, and by nine another couple had joined us and we were off. Fifteen of us. I glanced surreptitiously over the side to see if we were sinking. Wind from the NW at ten knots and not a cloud in the sky. Bobby winked at me as he went below. He'd pump the seas dry for $7.50.

There were no signs of the eagle. We saw the nest, all right, but Mark thought maybe we had scared them away. One couple obviously didn't believe there had been any eagle. I caught the word "gimmick." What did they think? The kid was in my employ? When we hit the swells past Bald Porcupine, a dumpy middle-aged woman, her face strained and pale, started toward the cabin doors. I stopped her just in time. If she wasn't feeling well, she'd be much better off lying on the deck, I assured her. "Some fun," her expression seemed to say as she climbed over the others and plopped herself down.

The Spivaks and their friends were sunning themselves on the cabintop, but the others, except for the seasick woman, were just sitting stiffly in the cockpit, as if in a dentist's waiting room, or on the subway. One grimly serious-looking man, Seasick's husband, I gathered, had hardly looked up from his New York Times since we left the dock. Another man, unfortunately just to windward of me, had just lit his third cigar of the trip. After a while, I, too, found myself concentrating on the middle distance, a vacant stare directed somewhere between the bow of the boat and the horizon—the traditional gaze of the sea captain, I realized with some shock. For half an hour the silence was broken only by the murmur of voices up forward, occasional moans from the deck and the jangle of Bobby's radio.

Suddenly the radio clicked off and Bobby came out. "Whew," he said. "Like a furnace in there. Thought I'd try the water." Everyone's eyes followed him as he walked to the bow. He dove in and then, faster than it seemed possible, he was standing upon the stern rubbing himself vigorously with a towel. "See over there?" he said, pointing with one arm at the tip of Ironbound. "Supposed to be treasure buried in that cave. Only can get at it at dead low tide, though."

The Times was dropped and a woman who hadn't said anything at all until then asked what the tide was now. Even the seasick woman raised her head off the deck and stared over at us. Luckily, the tide was too high. The story need not be tested. But that didn't seem to matter. They were all off and running, trading tales of treasure.

One of the men pulled out his key chain to show the golden doubloon he had found two winters ago on the beach near Daytona. If you really wanted to make a killing, the thing to do was get one of those mine detectors from Army surplus, he said. He'd be a rich man now if he'd thought of that at the time. But he hadn't the brains to go about it in a scientific way, and now he doubted if he could find the place. There was a fellow who made a good living just off the loose change that fell out of people's pockets, though. He'd talked to him last winter in St. Augustine, even watched him work the beach. Some day he'd be bound to hit it big. It just stood to reason with all the stuff that had been washed up for all these years, or buried by the pirates.

Bobby rowed the Spivaks into Seal Cove, just past the tip of the island, and when he got back he threw in a few more local stories. We sailed past the heron rookery and all the way round Ironbound without anyone in the cockpit so much as glancing out at the cliffs, but by this time I'd taken my cue from Bobby and when I thought they'd run out, I shifted the subject to the $150,000 house that was just barely visible from here on Yellow Island: the sunken purple bathtub that graced one of the three bathrooms, the walk-in fireplace in the living room, the price thirty to forty thousand dollars— I'd heard. I was so busy talking that I didn't notice there was one less person I was talking to. I turned my head in the direction of the scream, and there was Seasick coming out of the cabin, her wet slacks sticking to her ankles. "We're sinking!" she cried. "There's water all over in here!"

The secret was out. I was a proven fraud. I'd be laughed, stoned perhaps, out of town. I half closed my eyes, and then I heard Bobby's voice: "Gorry! I forgot to shut it off," and I saw him push past the woman in the doorway and before anyone else had a chance to look, he was back again. "She's okay now. Thanks a lot, lady. You sure saved us." And then to me, in a voice just loud enough for everyone to hear, "Sorry, Captain. Forgot to shut off the sea cock after I cleaned up in there."

I looked around to see how the rest of them were taking it, and the man with the doubloon gave me a sympathetic smile and a shake of his head, as if to say, "Kids. What are you going to do?" And I heard myself say, rather gruffly, "Well, pump ship, Bobby!" And to the woman who was still standing by the cabin doors, "Lady, if you're interested there's a job for you: crew watcher. Doesn't pay much, but..." And she smiled, and there were a few laughs and my stomach had come back into place, but what I was mostly thinking about was Bobby. To entertain them like that and then come up with that whopper. What a kid! But that was close. Too close. We'd have to work out some signals or something.

It wasn't much of a job to direct the group's interest back again to the subject of the house. One of the men pronounced that even at sixty thousand, the place would be a steal, and when I explained to them that the whole island was included, about five acres, he took out a pad and pencil and wrote it all down. Bobby came out about half an hour later and pointed out the smuggler's cave on long Porcupine Island, and we could easily have gone on like this for hours, but by then it was time to go back. So, we let down the sail and chugged sedately into Bar Harbor, much lively chatter advertising that there had been good times all around, crowds of prospective passengers, I hoped, taking it all in, from the dock.

The Spivaks' friends were the last to leave. The man handed me a ten dollar bill and with a smile told me to keep the change. The extra four dollars was for going in so close to the cliffs. If the shots he took of those herons came out, herons I hadn't even seen, he'd send me some. There were six people signed up already for the afternoon sail, and it was only twelve-fifteen. If we kept going at this rate, we might actually get rich after all.

I gave the four dollars to Bobby, who was pumping again.

"What's that for?" he said.

"The guy tipped us for seeing those herons. I figure you should get it. The brain work, that's extra, isn't it?"

Bobby grinned. "Thanks," he said. "From now on, though, we'll split it. Okay?"

"Fine," I said. "Even Stephen."

6

Lobster Picnics

The lobster picnics always had a festive quality about them, but then I was fortunate, for I had found out at the beginning that people had a better time if they were allowed to do all the work. I learned this quite by accident, and strictly from necessity. The second time we went out there were ten people along, and I was alone, Bobby being indisposed. I'd been doing everything, and when one of the men offered to row everyone ashore—three trips in our small dinghy—I did not protest. By the time he came to get me, the wood had been gathered and a fire started. I put the mystic amount of water into each of the two lobster pots and placed the cauldrons on to boil. "Anyone have a watch?" I asked, and the man who answered was put in charge of timing the lobsters.

"Can I do anything?" another man begged me.

"You want to melt the butter?" I said. He was overjoyed.

Everything was taken care of. Another man had assigned himself the task of feeding the fire. The women set out paper plates and forks and distributed piles of potato chips. It crossed my mind that if I approached it in the right way, I might be able to get someone to think it an honor to pump out the Scatt, but I decided not to risk that and rowed out myself on the pretext of getting an extra sweater. Twenty minutes later I had most of the water pumped out, and the crowd was chomping away at the feast by the time I got back. When I returned them all to the dock an hour or so later, the butter man slipped me a five dollar bill. "That's for letting me have so much fun," he said. And he really meant it. He'd been stumbling over the rocks all during dinner filling up our butter cups and making sure we all had enough and that it was still hot. He joked about always having wanted to be a maitre d', and we called him Francois and snapped our fingers for his attention. I got twenty bucks in tips that night. The passengers liked being useful. They enjoyed running the show themselves. For a while it was their island, their boat, their party. That's what it was all about. Doesn't every kid want to be a fireman or a truck driver at some point in his life? Wouldn't everyone love to run a subway for half an hour, or stand behind the wheel of the Queen Mary, even if it was only while the tugs were taking her out of her berth? They weren't being just passively entertained. They were participating in an adventure.

There was also a primitive element to the whole business that seemed to have universal appeal. Bashing the lobster claw open with a rock, letting the plate blow away and using the smooth ledge instead, dripping the succulent meat into the butter with your fingers, wiping your hands on your pants, throwing the shells onto the beach for the tide and the seagulls to take. All of this in the twilight of a fading sunset. You can't groan with the pleasure of fullness and throw the garbage over your shoulder when you're at a restaurant. There is a kindly savage in all of us that delights in tearing his food apart with his own hands and in the open air.

Without the slippery rocks on the beach, there would have been no challenge to the landing parties. A wet pant seat is an excuse to stand by the fire. You are busily occupied, yet doing nothing: the perfect conditions for contemplation. After the feast, when you wash your hands and face off in a tidal pool, or in the sea itself, you are indulging in an orgy of cleanliness. Your eyes smart from the campfire, and you may eat part of your dinner on the run, but your sweater smells of wood smoke for days afterwards. The fire itself cheers more deeply than its heat can ever penetrate, and makes a magic lantern of the night.

We would always put up the sail on the way to the lobster picnics, even when there was no wind and in spite of the fact that the island I chose was not more than a mile or so away. The very creaking of the pulleys made it seem as if we were entering unexplored territory. Even when Bobby or Lucy or some other helper was along, I always made use of the others as much as I could as soon as I found out what people actually liked. And, of course, this applied to the day sails too from then on. They would learn how to furl the sail and bundle it neatly in between the gaff and the boom before tying on the stops. The anchor man would discover how much scope to let out and what it felt like on the rope when the hook finally grabbed. There was always competition to see who would row the dinghy.

If we got to The Hop, or Sheep Porcupine, or wherever we were going, early enough and the tide was low, I would send off parties to dig clams or pick mussels while others explored the island and some even took a swim. If I could have arranged that they capture the lobsters themselves, it would have been even better. The hunt, the kill, the fire and then the feast. I learned how to stay out of things and, like a good English lord, let the house party run itself.

On the way back, there was often singing. Sometimes I would start it: "White sands and gray sands. White sands and gray sands. Who'll buy my white sands?" And if they liked that I would teach them other rounds that were more difficult, and often we would come in accompanied by the passionately sad swellings of "Oh, Absalom, my son, my son...," and the three or four who had been caught up in this would not want to leave; and we would sing it together once more through after the others had left, and if there was no moonlight sail, we might stay on and sing more rounds, though none could top this one, we always agreed.

Sometimes the moon rising from behind the island as we left it would stun us into silence, or it would be the stars themselves that would overwhelm us. A boy and girl would move off in the direction of the bow. A few might seek the warmth of the cabin which was mostly dry after the pumping. The rest of us, more often than not, would be caught up in what eye or ear could hardly contain, the pulse of waves on a distant shore; the roar and gravel-throated retreat of the surf on a shadowy point as we passed close to it; the ever-changing silhouette of trees against the sky and island shapes that seemed to rise and fall, too, with the tide.

By the time we reached the dock at Bar Harbor, usually a little late, there was almost a family feeling among us. If the moon was near its fullness and the night warm, I would be busy getting ready for the moonlight sail. Often, after we'd pushed off from the dock again with the new group, I'd look around and see that half the faces were familiar. Yet what was surprising in that, really? Who ever wants anything good to end?

7

Before the Mast with Admiral Morison

I was standing on the float, practically at attention, waiting for the great man to arrive. He would probably take one look at our boat, dress me down in no uncertain language, demand his money back (a week's groceries!) and inform me that his lawyer would see me in court. How could I have made the mistake of telling a biographer of Columbus, not to mention the official historian of the U.S. Navy, that the Scatt was a suitable vessel for him to charter for the day? Why couldn't I have just said no? Wait until he found out the motor didn't work, and that he wouldn't be able to talk over the sound of the radio. If the wind failed, he might even have to take his turn at the oars.

But it was too late for all that. Here they were, Admiral Morison and party, unloading picnic hampers and extra clothing from the station wagon that had just brought them the forty miles over from Northeast Harbor to Hancock Point. And there was the Admiral himself striding down the wharf toward me. At least he wasn't in uniform, only the typically eccentric costume of the aristocratic Northeast Harborite—Navy blue baseball cap, double-breasted blue flannel blazer with brass buttons, a white scarf, that was probably silk, at the throat, gray flannels bagging over dirty white sneakers. He was a large man, robustly denying his seventy-some years, his eyebrows bushy, his blue eyes penetrating, as he charged down the gangway.

"Fine day!" he shouted. "Trowbridge? Morison here." He crunched my hand in his. "Let's get right off, shall we? We're a bit late."

He hardly glanced at the boat, and seemed

pleased at the thought of sailing right off from the dock. "Here. I'll take the throat," he said to Tessa, crew for the day. Together they raised the sail.

"Cast off!" I shouted, and they jumped to do my bidding. Only after we were underway did he get round to introductions. Mrs. Morison was a fifty-something, conventionally pretty woman who appeared to be permanently, though attractively, flustered. Denney was the name of the well-tanned, elderly, horsey-looking couple who had come with them.

"Southwest," the Admiral said, taking note of the wind. "We can sail there and back again on a broad reach."

We were headed for deserted Turtle Island, ten miles away. The plan was to have lunch en route, go ashore for awhile afterwards to walk (or nap) it off, and then sail back again. We were two-thirds of the way there when Mrs. Morison brought out the lunch hampers. There was fried chicken, deviled eggs, a mixed salad, potato salad, buttered rolls, coleslaw, rolled up slices of ham and fresh cherries for dessert—all unwrapped, or unbuckled, or untied from smooth-looking leather boxes or shiny silvery tins all smelling delicious and looking like something from a magazine ad.

But first cocktails: a shimmering silver shaker of extra-potent Morison Daiquiris and little silver "glasses" were extracted from a pigskin attache-case-looking bar. The Admiral wet his lips as the cup was passed. "Won't you join us?" he said politely. I passed on the cocktails but could not say no to the food. Tessa was practically drooling.

After Mrs. Morison had served our lunch, she brought out another hamper filled with iced drinks—beer, Cokes, Orange Crush, the works. The Admiral, who had belted down two stiff ones only minutes before, accepted a bottle of beer with a broad smile. With one hand on the wheel, he drew a knife out of his pocket, the Boy Scout variety, extracted the bottle-opener with his thumbnail, removed the bottle cap, threw the knife overboard and put the cap into his pocket.

"Sam!" his wife remarked.

The Admiral grinned boyishly. "That's the third one I've lost this summer," he said. "That's why I buy 'em by the box."

By the time we reached the cherries, Tessa had entered a sort of fog. Three times she filled her plate. At last she refused. For the first time in her life, she had had her fill of perfect cherries. "Keep the rest for later," said Mrs. Morison kindly. And after some persuasion, she did. No one else wanted them, and they would just go to waste. There were two pounds of cherries at least.

When we reached the island, the Admiral rowed his party ashore, giving us a chance to pump. The water was well over the floorboards, so, as the wind had strengthened, I put in a reef. Half an hour later the Morison party returned in jovial spirits from their brisk walk around the island.

"What's this, Trowbridge?" said the Admiral as we pulled up the sail. "Afraid of a little spray?"

Intimidated, I took the reef out. Luckily we were headed pretty much downwind. Nevertheless, Tessa went below to her "radio" soon after we were off, and stayed there until we were halfway home. The Admiral was enjoying himself mightily. "A fine vessel," he said, straining to hold down the wheel.

I knew we couldn't go on like this for long. Each time a strong puff hit I could practically hear the water rushing in. Finally, I decided to act. "We'll have to put that reef back in," I barked. "Prepare to lower the sail."

The Admiral brought the Scatt up into the wind. We were sailing again when Tessa appeared at the cabin doors. Her face was red and wet with sweat, and I could see water sloshing over the floorboards and around her ankles.

"There's water down there," said Mrs. Morison. The Denneys looked over her shoulder. "We're sinking!"

she cried.

The Admiral left his post at the wheel and peered into the cabin. "Nothing to worry about, my dear. It's an old boat. Leaks a bit. They all do." He took off his coat and scarf and rolled up his sleeves. "Let's have that pump, young lady," he said. Forty minutes later he had bailed her dry.

With a double reef in the sail, the Scatt maintained an even keel and I began to relax. Perhaps, against all odds, everything was going to turn out all right. Mrs. Morison and the Denneys appeared calm, and the Admiral looked happier than ever back at the helm again for the last mile.

We rounded up alongside the float in good order and Tessa and I lowered the sail.

"I like the Scatt," the Admiral said, taking me aside before following the others up the gangway. His ice-blue eyes seemed to narrow. I felt my stomach sink as I waited for his "but." Now he was going to give it to me. "She's not like these modern yachts," he continued, boring into me with his eyes. His left hand slid into his inner coat pocket and out came his wallet. "A little something extra," he said, handing me two large bills. "A real ship," he went on, almost to himself. "No fancy geegaws."

8

Wind

The moment I woke up and heard the wind I knew I should stay in bed and do something else that day. It was blowing hard. Not really hard—fifteen to twenty knots, I guessed—but hard for six o'clock in the morning. For the past week, though, we had had nothing but fog and rain. Twice we had gone over to Bar Harbor anyway, on the chance that the weather would clear by afternoon or that we might pick up a few hardy types, but there had been a slow drizzle all day both times and we hadn't made a cent all week. Today was beautiful, crystal clear, with high cirrus clouds racing out of the NW. September weather!

I was half dressed when Lucy said, "You're not going, are you?"

"Sure. What do you mean? It's finally cleared," I heard myself say as I pulled on a sweater. It had gotten cold, too, in the night.

"But the motor's not fixed yet."

"The wind'll be with us. It doesn't matter. And we'll be able to use it on the way back."

The generator had burnt out on the last trip over, and I had left it in Bar Harbor to be fixed. I'd called yesterday about it and it was ready. No problem with that, and anyway, who wanted a motor when you could get there in half the time by sail? "We'll put in a reef. It'll be all right. Anyway, Tessa's dying to go." Even as I said all this, though, and was on my way to the kitchen, I knew she was right. I'd gotten the sign the second my eyes opened, that unlocated nervous feeling you have whenever you're about to do something you know is foolish. You were pretty sure you were going to do it, anyway. You were doing it, but at the same time watching yourself, sort of, waiting, half hoping that something would come up to stop you.

I was putting the coffee water on when Lucy came into the kitchen. "Clint, please! Don't go! Look at that wind."

There was a white pine about twenty-feet high outside the window. It was bending over to the left, jerking around as if trying to pull free. The bay was covered with whitecaps. But it was just a good wind, I kept telling myself. A good, strong wind, not a storm or anything.

"Look, I'll put two reefs in. What are you so worried about? You know she doesn't leak as much going with the wind."

Tessa, who'd been dying to take Bobby's place, especially since that day with the Morisons, appeared— clearly excited. Not the best day for a substitute, I thought, but she could manage it. Bobby had begged the day off, fed up after a nothing week. His parents had been pushing him to go lobstering with his brother and stop working for no pay.

"I'll call the weather, all right? If there's a hurricane or something coming, we won't go."

The phone was over by the window, and while I waited for the Coast Guard to answer, I stared out past the pine tree to where the gulls were riding above the spruces at the edge of the field halfway down the hill. Balanced there, stationary almost, they would tip a wing imperceptibly and swoop off toward the water in graceful, deliberate arcs. The harder the wind blew, the easier it was for them to fly. Suddenly I was dying to get going. Even with a reef in, the Scatt would plane in a wind like this. It would be all I could do to hold down the wheel.

When I was a kid, we always used to go out on days like this. My father and I, sometimes my mother and I, would drag the dinghy down the beach, half swamp it in the breakers and row out to the White Seal, the nineteen-foot sloop we had had for as long as I could remember. We'd go out deliberately in weather like this, and worse, and sail around with only the jib up if it was really stormy. Usually, though, we'd just take off with maybe a reef in, haul in the sheet as tight as we could and tack upwind for half an hour or so, getting soaked, holding her down until the water began pouring over the lee rail into the cockpit and only then letting the sheet out enough to spill some of the wind and straighten her up. We'd both be sitting way out on the edge of the deck, leaning back as far as we could, one hand on the six-inch gunwale that ran around the little cockpit. Balanced there like this, the lee rail just under, you could look down over the side and see the whole red knife-edge of the keel just a few inches below the water. I remember once, when we had her going like this, I edged myself carefully over the side until my foot touched the keel itself, and I stood there, holding on to the gunwale with one hand, and was able to lean out an extra few feet by doing this, get that much more weight out over the keel and so delay the moment when the sheet had to be slipped to save us from filling up and sinking.

We'd get her going wing and wing on the way back, trying to put her into a plane, but with that keel we never could quite manage it. Her nose would start to go under and we'd have to give it up. One time, when I was out on her by myself, I thought she was starting to plane, and then I had to pull the sail in to stop her mast from breaking. It was scary to see her mast, four to five feet above the stays, arc forward suddenly and then lurch back again.

I'd gotten the Scatt to plane that first day we took her out in Mantoloking. It had lasted only a moment, and then we were at the mooring in front of my mother-in-law's house. Suddenly there was a slow, steady, swishing, like the sound the line makes going through the ferrules when you cast a dry fly fishing for trout. It was a weightlessness, the hull rising out of the water as if it were about to fly, and then you would be going just a little faster than the wave, outracing it, running there in front of it for maybe fifteen seconds, until you hit the trough. There was a sense of having stopped, and then you were picked up by the next wave and you'd sweep ahead again toward this breathless, time-suspended, easiest and most peaceful of moments. The only time the wind had been strong enough to do this since that first day was when we had to fight it sailing across Casco Bay.

Coming back that evening would be rough, I thought, my eyes focusing once more on the jerking pine tree in front of me as the dull monotone of the Coast Guard voice came to an end. Even with the motor, it would take at least two hours unless the wind went down. "Small craft warnings, twenty to twenty-five knots." Just what I thought. I looked over at Lucy, but she was serving up the bacon and eggs, her face hidden from me.

"I wish you wouldn't go, just the same," she said. She'd given up, though. I could tell. And anyway, the vision of the Scatt planing before me all the way across the bay was all I could think of now.

* * *

There was a Wee Scot sailing around in the harbor. It wasn't even tipping much I noticed as we walked along the pier toward the float. Of course, the harbor was pretty well protected from anything from the north, but still, they probably weren't going to sail around just in here. A Wee Scot! In the Sorrento handicaps they'd always give the Wee Scots about an hour's head start over the other boats, but they were still the ones that had to be towed in if the wind dropped, or rescued if it was at all rough. They were tubby and small and unsafe and slow. I'd sailed past them plenty of times in the White Seal, watching them bob uncomfortably in a one-foot sea, feeling incredibly superior for my extra four feet and sleek lines.

When I was very young, about seven, I think, a boy from the Point had drowned in one of them. Of course, he'd gone out too far. It wasn't entirely the boat's fault. But still, whenever I saw these squat little sloops, I thought of him. The boy was about eighteen, and the story was that his family had refused him the car to go to Cranberry Island for a dance and so he'd sailed over in his Wee Scot, fifteen miles against the wind. It had taken him all day. He'd started back about one in the morning and apparently capsized. It was assumed that a squall had hit him—it was always puffy just under the mountains there—that he'd tied the sheet or just hadn't seen it coming. Anyway, his body was found the next morning on the bar off Bald Porcupine. There was no flotation in those days and his Wee Scot must have just filled and gone down.

We got into the dinghy and I rowed us out past the other boats to where the Scatt was moored. It was a little windier out here, but there was still nothing to worry about. Further out, though, you could see dark patches in the water when a squall hit, and over by Bean Island, a mile or so away, it was all whitecaps. It didn't look too bad, though, and I wondered whether we should bother with the reef. It took a good twenty minutes to put in. One reef. I'd put one in for Lucy's sake and just to be extra careful. We could always shake it out again once we saw what things were like.

But what a day it was. No trace of moisture in the air. The mountains, ten miles away, beyond Sullivan, were etched into a profile of greens and blacks and looked as if they fringed the bay.

As I sat on the cabin tying in the reef points, the Wee Scot sailed over to us and I saw that it was the Parrot boys. Hadley, their father, had bought the most beautiful forty-five-foot ketch I'd ever seen for ten thousand dollars the year before, and I admitted to envy. He was about thirty-five and had already sailed to Nova Scotia and back this summer.

"Your father out today?" I yelled over to the boys.

"No. Mom doesn't like it when it's rough. There're small craft warnings. You heard?"

"So what are you doing out?" I yelled back, remembering Hadley's description of his sail back from Halifax—he had only the storm jib and the jigger set for two days, and had told me he was scared as hell most of the time and that his wife had had it with long cruises like that.

"We're just sailing around in here. You going over today?"

"Ayah," I replied, speaking in the vernacular.

"Good luck," the older boy shouted as he jibed the little boat around our stern and headed back toward the float, he and his brother perched like two gulls on the raised deck, holding her down as much as they could in the sudden puff that had hit them.

Tessa finished pumping just as I was done, and we pulled the sail up to check the reefing. "Okay," I said. "Cast off." Once we got down by Bean Island, I'd bring her around on the other tack, I thought, but I sure as hell wasn't going to jibe her. "Crazy kids," I said to Tessa. "Did you see that?"

We moved off, gently at first, sweeping easily and with hardly a sound past the other boats and out into the bay. The first puff pulled her over a little, and I could see the green underside of her bow wave form itself beneath the sail, hear her now, the waves chunking lightly on her barely raised hull, the wave at her bow swishing off in a clean arc to the right, but I was hardly aware of any pressure on the wheel. Reefed down like this, the Scatt lost her monumentality, looked a little absurd also, almost ugly, in fact, with her gaff three feet below the crosstrees, and her mast, towering above her cut-down sail, naked and useless. We would be out in the real wind in a minute, though. Wait and see how it is, I told myself. If she doesn't look so good with a reef in, still, she may need it.

The wind was picking up, no longer coming in puffs but steadily. There were small whitecaps all around us and I could feel everything beginning to pull together. The strains, the tensions, were all balanced fore and aft sailing downwind like this. It was easier on her, this motion, easier on her than any other, for the keelson, rather than the ribs and planking, took the wrenching force of the mast, and the back stay anchored her down so that there was no play in her at all. The only sense of strain was at the wheel, the fight with the rudder to keep her downwind, for, of course, she wasn't perfectly balanced and had a tendency, always, to come up into the wind. The old square-riggers, that was the secret, I suddenly realized, looking at that quivering back stay that it was so important to get tight; nothing off balance at all. No fear of jibing, either. You could probably steer them by dragging a pole over the side, like a canoe, if the rudder broke. No wonder they could sail through the roaring forties without fear, could circumnavigate the globe as a matter of course. They followed the Trades, sailing with the wind around the world. Their masts were held in place by hundreds of stays, and the oak of their keelsons was as solid as the ground itself under their spruce trunk masts.

"Come on, Dad, take out the reef," said Tessa.

"Not yet," I said. I was surprised to see that we had already passed the western tip of Bean Island. It was time to bring the Scatt around on the other tack. Though we were moving right along, we weren't breaking any speed records, that was for sure.

"Ready about," I said. I let the wheel go and started to haul in the mainsheet.

Tessa's chair tipped off balance as the Scatt suddenly heeled over sharply, and she scuttled out of it and climbed up onto the high side, grinning.

"Loosen that back stay, will you?" I shouted as I

91

brought the Scatt into the wind and pulled in the slack on the starboard back stay. I cleated it and then we were downwind again on the other tack and heading for Bar Harbor, moving a little faster than we had before, it seemed to me. We were getting free of Hancock Point now, and into the full strength of the wind. The waves were beginning to pick up, from two feet or so to at least three feet in the last few minutes, and we were pitching as well as rocking in a slow, heaving motion from side to side as first the bow and then the stern crested on the waves. We would roll to the left. The rudder would come out of the water a foot or so, and then I would feel it in the wheel as the Scatt tried to pull off to the right, pitching down the wave, reaching her top speed, and then we would feel the wave pass slowly under us and the bow would begin to rise, pushing up walls of water twenty feet to either side, rising fiercely, it seemed, from its own counter-surf and then hiss to what felt like a dead stop as it reached the crest. Poised there, it would seem to hesitate before it tilted to the right; and then, there, just behind us, at eye level, the next wave would be curling, breaking toward us as we lay there, our stern only six inches out of the water, seemingly helpless, waiting to be swamped.

No matter how many times you'd experienced it, there was always the sense of escape each time the wave came at you and then, instead of crashing over you, would raise you into its breaking mouth, lift you softly into itself and then above itself, high into the air, as if to hurl you before it, and you would start to roar down its side once again. If the wind were strong enough, this was the moment that you might rise into a plane. You felt it about to happen, in the wheel—the force of the wave, the speed of the hull—you felt the wave itself, how strong it was, for if you were going fast enough, it did hurl you.

I remember the look on my mother-in-law's face when she saw waves like these for the first time that day off Mantoloking. She had been positive they would break in on us over the stern, and would not be reassured, even after the third or fourth time they lifted us high above themselves. Instead she had simply turned away from them and fixed her eyes straight ahead at her rented house in the distance, grimly waiting out the ordeal. I, meanwhile, was trembling in a sort of ecstasy, standing at the wheel while the Scatt planed.

"A little more and she'll do it," I yelled out to Tessa, who was looking very excited. I was standing up now with each wave, turning the wheel to the left as the stern lifted so as to be ready to fight the tendency of the Scatt to veer off upwind, standing also as if that would give her the added boost she needed to suddenly surge ahead, lift her hull and ride the wave: surf on it, down it, plane over it and reach, just ahead of it, the smooth black stillness of the trough.

We couldn't quite do it though; and after a while it became clear that unless the wind got a good deal stronger, we weren't going to. We were well off the Point, about a third of the way across the bay, I guessed, and there wasn't much more time. In another half hour we'd be there.

"Tessa!" I yelled, pulling in the mainsheet, then I let the wheel spin out of my hands and lunged over to the halyards. "Hold the wheel there," I said. I lowered the peak, and when I could see that the gaff was roughly horizontal, let the peak and the throat halyards go at the same time; and then I grabbed the gaff and was tying it with a line loosely around the boom so that it wouldn't smash around too much while I took out the reef points.

"Keep her into the wind," I yelled as I started to pull at the half shoelace knots I'd used at the reef points. I'd tied the final rope, way out at the end of the boom, with a square knot, though, and as I fumbled with it, we lost headway, and if Tessa hadn't quickly cleated the mainsheet, the boom would have taken me with it out over the water. As it was, I could only just touch the deck with my toes. The knot finally gave, and she pulled me back from where I was hanging, all my weight in the wrong direction. "Good girl," I called out, and then, with the Scatt rocking so that we could hardly stand, side-on as she was to the waves, we prepared to raise the sail again. This was the tricky part, getting that monster up without being headed directly into the wind.

I tied the wheel all the way over. "You take the peak," I said. "We'll have to go slow." Wallowing here like this there was a danger of broaching. In a big sea— if the waves had been, say, twice again what they were now—there would have been no question about it; the first one would have broken right into us. The problem now was to get up just enough sail to give us forward momentum but not so much that the wind and the waves would combine to flip her over while she was dead in the water.

"Okay, pull her up...that's it. Hold it... Now! All the way!" The sail was up, and I was back at the wheel turning it down hard, and the Scatt was falling off, the sail not flapping quite so much, and then the lee deck was awash as the sail filled all the way. Suddenly we were flying, going a third again as fast as we had been before, and it was all I could do to get her down, spoke by spoke, so that we were headed for Bar Harbor and not way up towards Hulls Cove.

It was hard to believe how fast she was going, or how differently she felt now that she had the bit in her teeth. She was planing on every wave but I couldn't keep her straight. She would veer to the right, each time, no matter how far I got the rudder over before she made her wild descent. She was taking the wave, not like a body surfer but like some pro out to break a record, riding the big ones at Diamond Head, not taking them straight but keeping the tail of his board in that green cavern under the lip of the wave as it raced toward him sideways at twenty miles an hour. Riding there, twisting and turning to get the extra points, staying right there in the lip of that curled mouth that rose sometimes ten feet above him, balancing there on his board, trying to make it all the way to the beach if he could.

The Scatt was riding the waves, not I. I was hanging on, forcing her back each time to take the wave straight, and each time losing at the end, the spokes of the wheel bruising my fingers as they turned in spite of me, the Scatt careening off to the right and across the wave until, finally, she lost enough wind for me to get her headed straight again.

I caught a glimpse of Tessa's excited face as she sat up against the cabin housing on the high side, her feet braced against the motor hatch to keep her from falling during those plunges to windward. Though the Scatt was planing, there was no lightness to her movement now. She plowed across the waves, her bow awash, the water crashing up against the front of the cabin and breaking over it. And then I saw why, and yelled to Tessa and she started down into the cabin; but the water was at least a foot over the floorboards and I could see by then that it was no use.

The trouble was that I couldn't quite keep even with what was happening. I realized, dimly, that each time the Scatt veered off upwind, she was under the kind of strain that had opened her up before, but it took six or eight or maybe twenty of those breakaways for that knowledge to sink in. I saw, too, how huge the waves were—six or seven feet high at least—but somehow did not connect that with the screech of the wind in the rigging, with the obvious fact that the wind had at least doubled in strength in the last few minutes.

I suppose it was just as well it happened. If the wheel had not finally spun free from my hands, we might have sailed on until the Scatt filled and we drove her right under. As it was, she took that last great sweep down and then across a wave that made me giddy just to look at it.

For a second I thought I'd gone overboard. The seat was there, though, and I pushed up from it, out from the foaming whiteness that covered it and straight up, it seemed, toward the deck above me; and then I was lying on the deck, the gunwale digging into my stomach, staring down at the curve of the Scatt's centerboard just under the water ten feet below me, waiting for the Scatt to turn over. But she didn't. She came all the way up into the wind and the wave broke over the cabin itself and drenched us. Without saying a word, we got the sail down and managed to secure it before we lost our momentum and started to plow sideways and down the waves again. Though I was shivering, my head was clear now. I turned the Scatt downwind all the way until she was lumbering along at about two knots—sailing on the bare hull. Though we were almost half full of water, we were not swamped. We were about two miles from Sheep Porcupine, heading straight for the entrance to Bar Harbor and there was still time to plan what to do. Meanwhile, we could tie down the wheel and get some of the water out.

We bailed with buckets straight into the cockpit from the cabin, faster than the self-bailing holes could drain the water. In five minutes the waterline in the cabin had dropped an inch. Half an hour and we'd have it all out. But where had this wind come from? The sky was still cloudless. Yet without warning, the wind had suddenly risen to what must be fifty or sixty miles an hour. You couldn't look directly into it. The waves were blowing apart before they could break, spray driving like hail from one wave crest to the next so that the whole bay was one sheet of foam.

Tessa was pumping into the centerboard well now, I was sitting at the wheel, protected from the driving spray by my slicker, testing to see how much control we had over the Scatt. The wheel moved easily in my hands and I felt a new lightness in the Scatt now that she was pretty well bailed out. We could sail at about a thirty-degree angle to the waves, I had discovered. With an arc of sixty degrees to play with, we shouldn't have any trouble steering through the narrow passage between Sheep Porcupine and Bar Island. Turning maybe fifteen degrees to the right after that, we could get enough into the shelter of Bar Island to drop the anchor, and then we would be only a hundred yards or so off Bar Harbor and someone could come out and get us.

There didn't seem to be anything more to worry about, and I began to slip into a kind of euphoria. Here we were, sailing along so easily, just as we had at the very beginning, but without a sail and in what amounted to a hurricane. There was a grace to her motion, also, that I had never felt before, as if these monstrous waves were merely very low, smooth hills covered with snow and the Scatt a toboggan gliding in the slow motion of a dream up and over and down a landscape that perfectly suited her, on a voyage one might almost wish would never come to an end. I had always thought that running under bare poles before a storm must be one of the ultimate terrifying experiences, yet here it was and it seemed instead the most natural way to sail. The Scatt, too, seemed to have found her most essential qualities as a boat now that she was stripped of her burden of canvas.

The tide was low and still going out, I noted as we approached the tiny passage between the islands. Waves were breaking right over the reef that stood out from Bar Island on our right, and then I saw that there were combers all the way across the channel to Sheep Porcupine. We couldn't get through, I suddenly realized, and turned the wheel hard to the left. We'd have to go out around the other side of Sheep, out past the bell. Luckily, I could just barely head for that. If I'd waited any longer we would have been lost, up onto the rocks of Sheep Porcupine only a hundred yards in front of us, or over the bar, where, if we didn't rip the bottom out of her, we would swamp for sure and probably be pitch-poled, end over end, by what looked from here to be at least fifteen-foot breakers.

Stupid! Stupid! Stupid! There was six feet of water at low tide in the channel, seven feet now maybe. Of course, with a sea like this running, the waves would be breaking across it. There was a strong current helping us toward the bell and away from the pounding surf in front of us. The same current, though, would sweep us past Bar Harbor and out to sea. Anchoring was out of the question. This was the ocean passage and the water was a hundred feet deep, even if we could get into the lee of Sheep, or Bald Porcupine Island.

"Don't worry," I said to Tessa. "We're just going around the other side." But I was the one who needed cheering, not her.

I supposed we could go on like this indefinitely, out past the Cranberries, beyond Schoodic Point and out of sight of land. Maybe we'd hit Nova Scotia by tomorrow night, if I could keep her far enough off to the left. Maybe we could survive being blown hundreds of miles out into the Atlantic, where the waves would tower thirty feet above us. Maybe, eventually, this wind would blow itself out and we could sail back in again. Maybe there was nothing to fear if we kept our heads and let the Scatt take us where she would. My impulse, though, was to try and beach her on Ironbound Island as we went by, or on Turtle Island beyond it, if we missed that. It was too late now to crash her onto Sheep Porcupine, and the cliffs of Bald Porcupine made any kind of landing there impossible.

Tessa was pumping again now. I took a last look over at Bar Harbor as we scudded past Bald Porcupine Island. There were tourists over there looking at us. There was a fat middle-aged man standing right now in the shelter of the information booth, looking over at us and vaguely wondering what we were doing. He and his family were munching Tastee Freezes, were bored and disgruntled because at least one day of their week's vacation had been spoiled by this lousy weather; and suddenly all I wanted was to be him, was to literally stand in his shoes and have no greater vision of joy ever come to me than a warm house and a safe job.

Some part of me must have seen the boat, for after we had passed Bald Porcupine, I found myself looking back as if for something, and then I did see it for sure: a lobster boat, invisible for minutes at a time when it or we were caught in the trough of a wave, but at each crest closer to us. There were two men. I could see them clearly now, and one of them had a coil of rope in his hand. I yelled to Tessa and she ran forward, and the second time the man threw it, she caught the line, got it around the forward cleat, and then the line stiffened, and slowly, imperceptibly at first, we began turning back toward Bar Harbor.

* * *

"So, you sent them out?" I said to Lucy who was waiting at the pier.

"It didn't take much," she said, "when I saw that pine tree in front of the window blow right over flat, I knew I had to get over here. They wanted to wait for the Coast Guard, but they went right out when I told them how badly the Scatt leaked."

9

The Summer of the Whale

The whale came into Frenchman Bay in early August and stayed two weeks. He was estimated to be sixty feet long, and it was thought that the islands had trapped him. Right away he became a prime tourist attraction. We offered hawks, herons and ospreys as part of the daily fare. If we passed Bald Rock at low tide, we could count on seals. Porpoises, too, wheezed about us continually. The eagle supplied every second or third party with a special treat. But a whale! The Scatt was packed with tourists even on bad days.

Normally, we kept our distance. Anxious as people were to see the leviathan, they properly respected its powers and a quarter mile away was close enough for most of them. Binoculars and telescopic lenses bridged the gap well enough. But Bobby and I began to get restive. He must be an old whale, we thought. He spent an extraordinary amount of time resting on the surface of the sea. For the first three days he could be seen in almost the same spot—between Ironbound and Bald Porcupine islands. Even through the binoculars he looked more like an old tree trunk or an upside-down submarine than he did a relation to Moby Dick.

Tame. Peaceful. He just lay there. Was he sunbathing, vacationing, recuperating from some epidemic of the deep? Or did he just enjoy being the center of attention, like a faded movie star who sits on the same park bench every day and hopes to be recognized? Like Old Faithful, he would blow off steam every so often, the camera shutters would click and he would be immortalized on celluloid for the thousandth time. Then he would disappear below the surface and there would be much speculation about what he was doing and where he might come up again. For the first few times, this was exciting enough. You imagined him roaring along like an express train through the sea lanes, his jaws open, sweeping up the terrified fish. You imagined their fear, the futile scattering out of the way as he charged through the calm flitterings of their undersea world—a steam shovel-headed locomotive rounding the corner of the sidewalk, unaccountably there, fifty feet away, coming straight at you at sixty miles an hour.

He would be swimming blind, except for the blinking radar of his voice or whatever it was that told him of danger ahead, his beady red-rimmed eyes looking no bigger than golf balls on a putting green, seeing only what flashed dimly by them: mindless, sleepless passengers on a train without an engineer, gazing dumbly through foggy windows at a landscape ill defined and vaguely threatening.

His radar told him three hundred, one hundred, fifty feet. The red alert of land. Then he would raise his great tail and loop back upon himself, baffled, perhaps, at discovering how small his world had become but responding instinctively to the danger, his monstrous hulk suddenly curling into a "U" that would take the wings off any airplane that tried so tight a turn, tail whipping back and then rising into a kick that would shoot him upside down into the turbulence of his own wake—back to the other side of his cage.

For we never saw him come up. He would be under the water for an hour, maybe, and then he would be seen again, not far from where he had gone down, quietly lolling on the surface.

South, toward the open sea, there was one obstacle: Egg Rock. He must have headed that way sometime during the third night, and finding that barrier in front of him—not knowing that if he followed it to either side for half a mile he would be free, no more capable of such reasoning than a train would be of jumping the rails to avoid a head-on collision—he must have turned back on himself, hitting the half-mile channel between Sheep Porcupine and Burnt Porcupine islands just right. He must have thought that he was out of the maze now, when suddenly Bald Rock or Hancock Point loomed up ahead of him and he had to turn back on himself once again. Then he was really trapped: land on three sides of him and that wall of islands with only the one narrow, deepwater channel through which he might escape.

There were eleven of them on board: five young couples and a dignified-looking elderly lady of about seventy-five. She had been the first to arrive, and I'm not sure she even heard the conversation. The others had phoned ahead for me to save space for them, and when they finally came trouping down the gangplank at five after nine, she was up by the bow looking out at the islands, obviously annoyed at being kept waiting. They had driven up that morning from Camden, where they had heard about the whale from someone I'd taken out the day before. How close could we get, did I think? One of them had been filming nature shots all summer in hopes of making a documentary of the Maine coast. If he could get some really good pictures of a sixty-foot whale, that would cinch the deal. Before we had even cast off, he was talking about chartering the Scatt for three or four days in a row. Mostly he'd worked from the shore so far. I said I didn't know, we'd have to see, but I guess he could tell I was all for it. Of course he'd pay extra for getting in really close, within a hundred yards, say. Twenty-five dollars as a minimum? I nodded my head. The nice old lady couldn't have heard any of this, though, for when we got out past Bald Porcupine and the groans of disappointment went up, she didn't seem to understand. It was a beautiful day. There was a good breeze, and it had been a long time since she had last been sailing—since before her husband died fifteen years ago, though when he was alive they went out together often. A whale? She had never heard of such a thing in these waters. We'd certainly better keep a good lookout for it and not get too close.

Though we'd seen no sign of him on the way over that morning, I figured that either the whale had gone back out to sea or he was in the inner bay someplace. I pulled the sail in and headed for the eastern tip of Sheep Porcupine. It was blowing about fifteen or twenty knots, and even with the reef I'd put in earlier—I automatically put one in now for anything over ten knots—we were tipping a little and I could tell from the way she looked that the old lady was enjoying herself.

We weren't more than a quarter of a mile away when we saw him, lying up to windward of us, looking just like the ledges that jutted out from Bald Rock behind him—the same dark gray color, almost black, though smoother, much smoother, than any rock. He glistened there in the sun like some ebony carving, and then he spouted—a geyser of spray mushrooming into the air—and I yelled out, "Thar she blows!"

At first the old lady just looked startled, as if her husband had suddenly appeared from nowhere and called her name. When I turned on the engine and headed up toward the whale, I could see the shock on her face change to anger, as if she'd just realized that she was the victim of a press gang: and then, as if she were simply disowning us all, she took up her purse and brushed past Bobby, who was standing at the cabin doors, and went inside.

The others were wild with excitement. Larry, the boy with the movie camera, was filming away and yelling out for the rest of them to keep quiet, though what he was getting from here couldn't be very impressive-looking. And then I got the whale in the binoculars, and a chill went through me as I looked into his eye. It was the eye of something completely foreign, as if a cliff or a wave had an eye. It had no expression in it, though it seemed to be looking at us, waiting for us, you might even say.

I passed on the glasses and yelled out the orders to get the sail down. We were perhaps fifty yards away and I felt as if I'd been warned, somehow, not to go closer. Even without the glasses, we could clearly see the glistening brimstone of his back, his great tail darkening the water behind him. He was perfectly still. He did not seem to rise and fall with the waves at all, as if he were a fixture there, a ledge of rubbery, smooth rock risen from the sea floor. There was a suggestion of iceberg depths of whaleness beneath what we saw, yet the eye was only just visible from where we were and, without the glasses, it seemed more like a depression, a hole in his side.

And then, very slowly, he began to move—forward, and across our bow—the great cliff of his brow heaping the water in front of it into one giant wave. Then he started to sink, all at once, just like a submarine. The wave broke over his head, and at the same instant his body arced forward and the feathered tips of his flukes rose into the air, struck the water lightly and he disappeared. It wasn't even the full tail, just six or eight feet of its tip, but though it waved up and then down with the lightness of a lady's fan the air cracked with the sound of it and the wave, when it hit us, was a good foot high.

There were cries of disappointment. How soon would the whale be coming up again? An hour? "Time to head back, anyhow," I said, and told them to get ready to raise the sail. It was eleven-thirty. We'd be late coming in as it was.

We were on course for Bar Harbor and I'd just flicked the motor off, when not more than twenty yards behind us, we saw the whale. Everyone yelled with excitement. He was coming at us in shallow, rolling dives. I turned the wheel down to see if he were in fact following us, and he altered his course too. Back the other way. He came no closer, his great rolling hulk seeming to move in slow motion. What was he doing? Playing cat and mouse? I turned the motor on again, hoping the noise would scare him away—which it did. He was down longer, for a good ten minutes, and then, suddenly, off to starboard, not thirty-feet away, the great whale rose into the air and we saw for the first time the whole crooked line of his jaw. He kept coming, the whole length of him. He rose and rose, and then, his whole body in the air, he arched his back. For a fraction of a second he seemed to hang, weightless in front of us, and then he plunged straight down into the crater from which he had burst.

I had seen an oil tanker break apart once. She was docked, riding high in the water, when suddenly, she split at midship from one side to the other, both ends sinking immediately into the water, her torn center section rising into the air—an inglorious and somehow triumphal gesture. It sounded like the crack of doom from where I sat across the harbor, fishing. The tidal wave it caused almost swept me from the pier. This was something like that—only more magnificent.

We were all still staring at the water in a daze when the whale breached again, on the other side of the Scatt. Not as high this time, more like the leaping of some giant porpoise. "He thinks we're another whale," said one of the girls.

"Oh, oh! That could mean trouble," her boyfriend yelled out in mock terror, and everyone laughed.

I didn't really dwell on it, but I couldn't help imagining what it would be like if that great leviathan chose to rub his flank up against our side and nudge his urgencies, playful or not, along the fragile skin of our hull. From under the water we might look like another whale to him. He might graze us with his hump, or touch us with the edge of that tail as he dove under us. Accidentally. It could happen without his feeling it, even. Or he might suddenly raise his head high in anger or disdain and with one battering surge turn us into wreckage.

We were getting near to the passage between Bar

Island and Sheep Porcupine, and I was beginning to wonder what we would do if he actually followed us into Bar Harbor, when I saw the old lady standing at the cabin doors. "There's water all over the floor in here." And then she saw the whale and her expression softened. "He's like a big dog." She smiled, and I was sorry then she hadn't come out sooner, for that was the last we saw of him. A few minutes later we were going through the narrow channel. Of course, I realized, the whale would have been warned of the danger and turned back, baffled, perhaps, by the fact that we had kept going; would have had to turn back on himself with even greater speed than usual to avoid the rocks ahead.

10

In the Wake of the Whale

The whale caught all the tourists for us we could handle, and even after he left the bay the magic of his presence lingered on. Much as I hated to do it, we had to turn people away. Fifteen, I decided, was the maximum. Even at that, half of them had to be cooped up in the cabin each time we raised or lowered the sail. With people sprawled all over the boat like Sunday picnickers in a city park, it was risky enough coming about at all, so we sailed out and back again on one long tack. Even so, there were always one or two unable or unwilling to grasp this concept, no matter how carefully I explained it, always a few who seemed to want to be swept into oblivion by the boom. We didn't see the herons or the eagle, or much of anything else for that matter, except the water and the distant vistas of islands and shoreline, but that was what we had to pay for packing them in like this. At the wheel, I, of course, saw virtually nothing. I'd had to stand up on the seat and peer out over the crowd every so often, raising the periscope of myself above the surface of this human sea, just to get my rough bearings. Blind, I found that I could sail us fairly straight in open waters by looking behind us at the wake. It was a little like being a bus driver whose vehicle operated only in reverse. I stared into the rearview mirror and consoled myself with the knowledge that I was becoming rich.

The weather continued perfect—day after day, with steady but moderate southwest winds. Usually, I'd circle out around Egg Rock for the morning sail, the way the tourist boats did, and take the northbound line toward Hancock Point in the afternoon. Boring, but predictable.

I tried to take out no more than ten on the moonlight sail, and after a while I cut out those trips altogether, or just about. On one of the first of them, an elderly woman in high heels, who happened to be holding a can of beer in her hand at the time, was knocked down and almost overboard by the boom when the wind shifted and we unexpectedly jibed. I pictured looking for her in the black waters without even the benefit of a decent spotlight, and from then on I tried to insist that the passengers stay in the cockpit and remain seated. I avoided going out at all unless there really was a moon and it didn't look as if the wind would come up, but you could never tell just what was going to happen at night. Once a fierce wind came up after we had been out for about an hour, and there was a foot of water over the floorboards when we got back. That was another thing. It was almost impossible to keep people out of the cabin during those sails, particularly when it was cold. Fortunately, this time there were only two couples, and they splashed each other and drank beer and apparently had a fine time in what they must have thought of as their own private swimming pool, and I didn't even find out about it until we got in and they came sloshing out of the cabin and went guffawing off into the night.

I should have canceled the trip entirely, I suppose. People waiting for us at the dock were disappointed and sometimes angry when I explained we weren't going out that night. A well-known movie actress, the summer star of our local thespians, threatened to sue me for breach of contract when I wouldn't take her and her troupe out one windy night. I couldn't very well explain that I'd really be giving her grounds if I did.

In all of August I think we ran the moonlight sail only three times. I hated to turn people away, though, particularly on the day sails, and often wished we had a larger boat. I even considered using the dinghy for the overflow. Three could sit there comfortably, and I would offer them slightly reduced rates. Better yet, I could accept eighteen and then explain that everybody gets to spend half an hour in the dinghy at no extra charge. People were always begging to ride there anyhow. Why not make use of it? I could have towed a barge, run a floating crap game. I should have. I should have made hay while the sun shined. But instead I settled for one hundred and fifty to two hundred dollars a day and kept my fingers crossed. I was becoming conservative.

Only once did I break my rule, and that was when eighteen members of the Piper Cub Club of America flew into Bar Harbor, and they all wanted to go out on the lobster picnic. It was all or nothing, so I borrowed three life preservers and made an exception in their favor. Fortunately, there was not the slightest breath of wind and the engine was functioning. They swarmed aboard, every one of them loaded down with camera equipment, and I could hear the sea bubbling in the cockpit drains. One more person would have been too much. One more camera, maybe. Down we would have gone: glub, glub. Quietly, peacefully at first, getting it all on film. We motored over to the sunset side of Sheep Porcupine Island, only a half a mile away, but got back a little late at that, so much time did it take to get everyone off and then back on again. They loved it, though. They had a great time. With the extra lobsters they'd ordered and the tips, it came to one hundred and sixteen dollars. It was the high point of the summer for Bobby and me.

By the middle of August I was thinking big. Not only would we rebuild the Scatt (we had almost enough for that now), we would look around for another boat as well—a small schooner, maybe. Every year we would add another vessel to the fleet. By the time I was thirty I'd be the Aga Khan of Bar Harbor, and Bobby would be my general manager. I would spend most of my time christening ships and being interviewed by the newspapers. I would be too busy with financial matters to actually captain any of the boats myself, but occasionally I would appear on board as a surprise for the tourists, and I would make it a practice to toast each vessel when it left the dock on its maiden voyage of the season. There would be a little party, an item in the newspaper. And when they grew up, Paul and Patrick would enter the family business, working their way up as I had done. We should start right away on more sons. Two was hardly enough if you had a dynasty in mind.

I'd also decided that the Scatt had to have a new engine. A few days after the Piper Cub Club flew on, the motor collapsed. After we missed two morning sails in a row on its account, and with only two weeks to go, we decided to do without it. From then on we left the Scatt on a mooring in Bar Harbor overnight and commuted in Bobby's car. Oddly enough, we discovered that it was excellent advertising to sail our passengers right up to the dock instead of motoring in. "Look, Mommy! That boat's going to crash!" They'd come running over in the hundreds, it seemed, every time. Of course, every once in a while we'd make a mistake. Like the time we forgot to untie the stern line from the wharf. Luckily, the rope was old and we barely felt the jerk when it parted. What was impressive was how many times we did it just right. It wasn't easy. Getting most of the tourists down into the cabin so I could see where I was going as we came in was a feat in itself. I'd have to snake us through the armada of the local fleet and then, when I had a clear shot at the wharf, nose the Scatt up into the wind at just the right angle so as to bring her to a halt near enough to the float for Bobby to jump off with the mooring line. Not into the float, not past it and onto the shore or through the hull of another boat, but up to it. It took the kind of timing one expects only airplane pilots to possess, and I felt justifiably proud of my perfect record. Anyone can handle a motorboat, but a vessel that depends entirely on sail is another matter. It takes a special knack. And people realized it. A skipper like that you could have confidence in. As I say, not having a motor turned out to be very good for business.

A good reputation can hurt you, though. It makes other people jealous. We must have been taking business away from the tourist boats. At least I can't think of any other explanation for what happened. Who else would try to scuttle the Scatt? Fortunately, they didn't quite succeed. The Scatt was about half full of water when we got there that morning. I knew someone had tried to ruin us because one of the bilge plugs had been knocked out. If they'd done a good job and removed all four of them, we would have found her awash, and it would have cost us a full day to get her pumped out and cleaned up again. As it was, though, we'd arrived early and were able to pile them on for the morning sail as usual. The motor was shot anyway, so we didn't care about it being flooded. From then on we locked her up at night. We took it as a compliment, actually. Only the rich get robbed.

* * *

At twelve-fifteen on the afternoon of August 23rd, the governor of Puerto Rico and party (fourteen in all) got aboard the Scatt for a prearranged and strictly private afternoon sail. Since they were bringing lunch and starting a little early, I had agreed on the special price of sixty dollars and had already sold ten tickets to disappointed members of the general public for the next afternoon. The governor wore a white suit, and three of the women carried furs. Were they going to an embassy party afterward, or was this how the governor entertained visiting royalty on his private yacht? Lucy, who was replacing Bobby for the day, looked nervous, as she carefully checked some twenty-five thousand dollars worth of furs into the cabin. Today she would double as ladies' maid and pumper extraordinaire.

Although there was only a very light breeze, I had done my part by putting in a reef after we got in from the morning sail. We were drifting with the tide, the sail barely full, between Bar Island and Sheep Porcupine, when a woman of Cleopatrean elegance gestured in the direction of the sail in a way that clearly indicated what she thought of such caution. All at once I realized the enormous advantage the native has over the monolingual foreign visitor. I shrugged my shoulders and, smiling broadly, pointed toward the cloudless skies. Big wind. Come over mountain. Little boat. Much sea. I smiled more broadly, then puffed my cheeks out and blew in the direction of the sail, pointed again and mumbled something in the neighborhood of "Mucho areo." She turned on her heel, imperiously unimpressed, and motioned with her fingers for the governor to give her a cigarette.

There was much animated conversation while they unpacked the lunch, and I found it all very restful not being able to participate except through sign language. I'd been getting pretty bored giving the same little speeches every day. For once I could sit behind the wheel in silence, merely nodding and smiling foolishly when anyone addressed me. At one point, the governor, who was standing to my left, commanded the attention of the group, and gesturing in the general direction of Mount Desert Island, said something apparently commendatory about its beauty. Someone offered a toast, and they all drank with him out of tiny silver cups, while the governor held his Balboan pose. A few of them glanced in my direction afterwards, as if to say, "And this fortunate man. He lives among this beauty all year long. This is his home. Yet probably he has never looked at it, is incapable of appreciating the extraordinary resemblance it bears to the Greek Isles. Why can't he be content to spend his life here living off the bounty of this paradise? Why do they all want to go to New York and become electricians?"

"Viva America!" I said, raising my arm in the gesture of a toast, and they all laughed.

We turned back toward Bar Harbor after they finished eating. We hadn't gotten even as far as Bald Rock and it was only a little after two, but the tide wouldn't be high until almost three, and I knew we would hardly make headway against it. We didn't. The wind had dropped to almost nothing. I took out the reef in hopes of catching what little there was of it left. Though Cleopatra looked on with approval, her whole demeanor now suggested that the barge she sat on was no burnished throne. Yawning, she stretched out in the sun, lizard-like, and drifted off with the others into siesta time.

It was hot. Sweat dripped down my cheeks. The sail flapped idly, and we started to drift backwards in the general direction of the ledges off Bald Rock. What to do? It was too deep to drop anchor. I pictured myself sounding the general alarm as we bumped up onto the rocks, the governor and his crew scurrying over the sides in response to my gestures of command. I also imagined their inability to push the boat off in time, and, as a consequence, our having to sit it out together on the ever more sharply slanting decks until the tide released us at about three-thirty in the morning.

I went below for a quick conference with Lucy. She was lying down on a non-fur-covered section of the bunk and seemed reluctant to move. Of course there was only one thing we could do—row. After all, I explained, she had the easy job. All she had to do was steer.

I'd towed the Scatt short distances before, though it was Bobby who manned the oars when we brought her into the dock in the morning. Bar Harbor was about two miles off. If I pulled like a galley slave, I should be able to get us in before five. If the wind didn't come up by then, we'd have to skip the lobster picnic. I certainly wasn't going to feel like towing us back out again. Right now, though, it was good to be doing something. Out there in front of the Scatt, pulling at the oars, I felt the liberating effect of purely physical effort.

After five minutes of steady pulling, I was drenched with sweat and we seemed to be no further ahead than before. Running in place in your living room may be just as good for your lungs and legs, but it isn't the same as loping across open fields. The Scatt seemed to be made of lead. I might have been towing a dead whale. And I'd have to do this for at least another half hour before the tide turned and we showed some progress in the right direction. What a tub she was. How different from the White Seal; how graceful and responsive she had been.

We'd almost counted on it in those days—having to row in if we picnicked on one of the outer islands. We'd always mean to allow more time, but it would be four o'clock before we left The Hop or Yellow Island or one of the Porcupines, and by six the wind would almost always flutter and then die; and there we'd be, off the tip of Hancock Point, becalmed. If the tide were with us, we'd drift in around seven, but more often than not it was going the other way. We didn't really care, though. There were usually three or four of us in the boat, and if we were in a hurry, we'd take turns at the oars and be in by seven anyway. Sometimes we would just let ourselves drift backwards and wait for the tide to shift or the wind to come up. Most of the rounds I know I learned during those drifting hours.

Towing the Scatt, particularly with all these people aboard, was a tug of war. Even after the current began to slacken and I settled down for the long pull, it didn't look as if I could possibly make it all the way to Bar Harbor before dark.

The governor and Cleopatra were standing on the bow scanning the shoreline, and I heard him distinctly say to her, in perfect English, "No motor! Can you believe such a thing?" He hadn't paid me yet. He might refuse to now, might even make real trouble for me for getting them stuck out here like this. I had started to pull with greater vigor at the oars, when I saw the Coast Guard boat not more than three hundred yards away and coming straight at us.

Hallelujah! All at once I was exhausted, could hardly get up the energy to ship the oars before the Scatt slid up past me and the tow rope pulled me up against its side. My arms and back ached as if I'd been rowing for hours, and there was a painful rawness at the base of my spine. No one was looking at me, though. They were all on the port side, waving and shouting at the approaching boat, making as much commotion as if we'd been out for days, as if they really were being rescued.

Lucy was on the bow waiting for the line, but instead they pulled right up alongside. Chief Moon, all dolled up in his dress whites as if he were some visiting dignitary himself, stepped aboard and shook hands with the governor, and then, while one of his men got his tow line onto our forward cleat, he walked over to me, a clipboard in his hand.

"Courtesy inspection, Trowbridge. Thought I'd save time and run through it with you while we go in."

"Sure," I said. "Thanks for the tow. You want to count those life preservers over again?"

He looked at me as if I'd made a bad joke.

"I'm trying to go through the check list with everyone a few days before the new regulations go into effect, just in case there're some little things that still need to be done. Let's start with the radio. Where did you put it? Never mind. I'll find it."

The thing was, I simply couldn't talk for a minute. That crazy law. It did apply to us. When we'd gotten the notice in July we'd howled with laughter at the idea that we were to insert "fume-proof bulkheads between the engine room and the cabin areas." What did that mean, tack-up a sheet of plastic over the crawl space under the cabin steps? Surely they had in mind ocean liners or at least something the size of the tourist boats in Bar Harbor. Why on earth would they want us to have a two-way radio which, if I remembered correctly, had to have a calling distance of at least twenty miles and required a radio operator's license to run it? We'd thrown the letter away and thought nothing more about it.

Moon was coming out of the cabin, and I could tell by his face that there was nothing even to discuss. My insides started slipping away from me, and I suddenly knew what it felt like to be a criminal in the eyes of the law. If I'd been caught with a boatload of heroin, I couldn't have been looked at with greater disgust. "After tomorrow you're limited by law to six passengers," he said, and, pushing his way to the bow, signaled his boat to drop back and pick him up.

I was out of business. Six people was nothing. Eighteen crummy bucks for a half a day's sail? Thirteen more days. If they were going to wait this long, couldn't they have waited thirteen more days? My face was still burning, but now all I could think of was how absurd it was. If my boat was considered unsafe as a vessel, why did they let me take anybody? Six people I could drown, though, eight including myself and Bobby. But seven. That was going too far! And then I noticed that there were at least two inches of water on the floorboards in the cabin. Moon hadn't even mentioned that. He'd found me out. I was taking out tourists on a boat that leaked so badly that if you didn't pump it every minute she'd fill up on you, and he didn't care. He didn't care that my engine was kaput. These things weren't in the regulations. As long as you had a two-way radio aboard, the Coast Guard didn't care that you were perpetually sinking. What we'd been trying to hide all summer didn't matter to anyone, apparently. That we'd managed to get through it all without disaster was not important, not even interesting enough to condemn us for trying it. Moon must have waded through that bilge water, yet he had said nothing. What did he think, that we kept it that way on purpose? Well, if he didn't care, I didn't either. I turned the wheel over to Lucy and got out the pump. The governor and Cleopatra and the rest of them looked at me as if to demand an explanation, but I neither smiled nor nodded my head. I stood there in the doorway of the cabin pumping out bilge water before them all, my face expressionless, making no excuses for anything. Their coats were dry. The Coast Guard had rescued them. They'd get back on time.

11

Night Thoughts

I had no idea what time it was, only that it was still night and that something was wrong. There was a wailing in the distance. It rose to a shriek, then fell to a childlike murmur. For a long time I lay there in the dark and tried to ignore it. We'd been out late the night before, celebrating the end of the tourist business. In three days we'd be off to Florida for a restful, graduate school winter. I had thought our troubles were over.

The wailing sound in the distance wouldn't go away, though. I'd be just about asleep again, when, as if in desperation, it would rise to a shriek, and for a second I would hear it as something human. One of those strange nightmare seizures would take hold of my body and I would be wide awake, trying to catch my breath. It was the wind. I knew that. Nothing but a storm of some sort. But the third time it happened, I decided I just couldn't lie there any longer. I'd shut the window. Maybe then I could ignore it.

It was raining into the bedroom. The curtains were soaked and the floor felt wet and cold to my feet. The window was stuck, swollen with the damp. I stood there a moment before trying it again, trying to pierce the darkness. The rain beat in on my chest with sudden fury, and the walls trembled. Wet and shivering, I ran downstairs to call the Coast Guard. This was no ordinary storm.

There was a hurricane coming. It was seventy miles off Cape Small, and if it kept its course it was expected to pass through the Mount Desert area before noon. Houses situated in low-lying areas should be evacuated in case of flooding. Motorists were warned against fallen trees and the danger of high-tension wires on the road, and urged to stay where they were. Boat owners should secure extra lines to moorings and wherever possible to the shore, and keep their engines running. Under no circumstances were they to move their vessels. Winds gusting upwards of seventy miles an hour could be expected in the Mount Desert area by nine o'clock.

I would have to leave immediately. Though it was only five o'clock, it might take two hours to drive to Bar Harbor in this weather, and I wouldn't have a chance of getting out to the Scatt if it really blew. Luckily, I was on one of the heavier moorings—so the harbor master had told me, anyway. What I couldn't understand was why I was feeling so lightheaded and full of energy all of a sudden. It was the same sensation I used to have as a boy when I'd get up before dawn to go trout fishing with my father: the silence of the sleeping house, the darkness, the anticipation—it was as if I was actually looking forward to sitting out a hurricane on the Scatt. Perhaps I should get my father to come with me, or Lucy. But what could they do? And anyway, though I couldn't explain why, I knew I wanted to be alone. I got my clothes together quietly, made a quick breakfast, packed a few sandwiches and left a note for Lucy on the kitchen table. The clank of the frying pan on the stove, the sound the light switch made when I turned it on in the kitchen, every noise seemed preternaturally loud, but the house remained quiet. It was going to be a long day: the summer's last adventure.

12

Hurricane

There was a trace of light in the east, but it seemed only to increase the gloom. The spruces beside the road swayed and dipped with each gust. The rain-soaked shingles of the darkened houses glinted with the dullness of gun metal. Everything seemed to consist of interminable grayness as if the earth were covered by one enormous soggy sheet of newsprint. The wind whipped at the car with such savageness at times that I was forced to stop for fear of going off into the ditch. It took all my concentration just to follow that black ribbon of glistening tar that kept disappearing beneath a blacker sea.

I'd been trying not to think of the Scatt at all, but when a particularly heavy squall would hit, the boat would loom up before my eyes, her bow rising out of the sea, straining at her mooring line as if in a frenzy to shake it loose. I saw the cleat pulling the washers at the end of the bolts up into the oaken deck plate. With each lurch I could feel them dig in a little further, could hear the rasping tear of the nut stripping off, could imagine the cleat tilting forward and snapping the bolts like match sticks, the easy sweep of her bow now that she was no longer held... My hands would tighten on the wheel and then, as suddenly as it had come, the vision would pass. It was a tiny variation in the drumming of the rain, perhaps, or the windshield wipers clearing the glass in front of me for a second. There was a momentary lull as the squall passed, and the road ahead became visible once more. And then five or ten minutes later, it would come again, each time with the same absolutely unquestioned authority of an actual event.

It must have been blowing a good thirty or forty

knots by the time I got there, but there was a lobsterboat tied up on the lee side of the float, and I climbed aboard to see if the owner would take me out. I was in luck. He was just about to put his boat on her mooring. He and his son had been out earlier pulling traps, but he'd given that up pretty fast, and he supposed he was the only fisherman crazy enough to have gone out at all. Should have listened to his radio and taken the day off instead, he said, but at four o'clock it hadn't been all that bad and he didn't put much stock in these weather reports. It looked as if they might be right this time, though. He'd drop me off and then tie up and go home to bed. Wasn't he going to stay on his boat during the hurricane, I asked him. "What for?" he said. If a wind came up that was strong enough to bust his mooring chain, he didn't want to be aboard. If you had to pump, that was something else, but his boat was tight. We passed two powerboats that had their engines running already and then a big yawl I hadn't seen before that must have come in during the night. A figure waved at us from the cabin, one short salute of a raised arm, actually, and I wondered how he felt with a thirty or forty thousand dollar yacht like that to worry about.

It took us a while, but finally the familiar shape of the Scatt loomed up ahead in the dim light and they let me off. She was low in the water, so I got the pump out and in half an hour the floorboards were showing again.

Except for the screeching of the wind in the rigging, it didn't seem much worse than the usual storm. What was deceptive was that she was pitching so little. She'd yaw back and forth on her mooring, first to one side and then to the other, but there was no more up and down motion than there would be on a barge. I lit the stove, put on a pot of water for coffee and changed into some dry socks and boots. The rain was dripping through in a few places, but I'd found most of the leaks this summer and there was a whole section of bunk that was fairly dry. I snapped up my side of the table, made myself a cup of coffee and ate a sandwich.

The scene framed by the cabin doors was one I'd looked at a million times, it seemed: the glistening sheen of rain-washed paint, the stream of water that fell in a cascade of drips from under the boom, the tiny rivulet flowing first from one spoke and then another as the varnished wheel turned with the rudder, the dim sea and rain-drenched sky that disappeared as if behind a waterfall fifty feet away. I might have been in any one of a thousand harbors along the coast, cruising, waiting out a bad spell of weather. That was something Lucy could never understand about me, why I didn't care about going ashore when it was like this. And the times we'd been caught out in the rain and I'd have to sit behind the wheel for hours, all day sometimes. "Why are you smiling?" she yelled out at me once. "I don't understand you at all."

What could I say? I couldn't really figure it out myself. Each kind of weather had its own particular delight for me. I had never been able to explain to her how I had felt somehow intoxicated with joy during that shipwreck. For her it had been an ordeal, a test of endurance that she could not possibly have passed if she had not been given additional strength. She had been able to bail for eight hours without rest and the next morning had not even felt stiff. The wind had suddenly stopped and the seas were calm enough for us to row into the beach at Cape Small. The Hatfields' light had guided us. These were miracles to her.

The Scatt gave a sudden lurch. It was time to get the anchor line around the mast and tie it to the loop of the mooring rope and so bypass the cleat, then check the chafing gear. I groped my way forward on my hands and knees. I could hardly see ahead of me and the rain stung my face as if it were hail. The wind was at least twice as strong as it had been an hour ago, seventy miles per hour or near it. I pulled at the anchor line, but it was stuck. I'd have to go back down inside the cabin.

Just as I'd thought. The anchor line was pulled up against the under part of the deck, all tangled in the life preservers. I unscrambled the mess, and looking up noticed the timber that came back from the bow as far as the mast, that huge piece of oak through which the two heavy cleat bolts protruded, was split. I slid my fingernail into it to make sure. Was this something new or had it always been there? No way to tell. I got down on my stomach again and inched my way backwards out of the hole. Hurry! Hurry! Fasten that safety line around the mast before it's too late!

It took me twice as long as before to crawl up along that slippery deck. By the time I had the anchor line secured around the mast, the Scatt was taking water over the bow. Back in the cabin, I collapsed onto the bunk for a minute to get my breath before starting to pump again. Either the wind had shifted or the tide had risen up above the bar. If the wind had come around to the south or southeast, we'd be getting the ocean swells. Not directly. But I'd seen Bar Harbor in a southeaster and I knew that if it got bad enough, and nothing broke first, the Scatt would pull herself right under. Waves would wash over the cabin and into the cockpit; the self-bailing holes wouldn't do any good in a boarding sea; the water would flood in through the cabin doors; and when she got that heavy, something would have to give. We'd be up on the rocks of Bar Island, beaten into wreckage in ten minutes, and I'd be lucky if I could even get off her.

There were about three inches of water over the floorboards when I got up to pump. I thought I heard voices, but how could I have with the wind howling like a banshee and the slatting of the halyards? A second later there was a crashing jolt and at the same time a wrenching, splintering sound from the bow. All I could think of was that the next wave would lift us, and whatever it was that had happened would happen again, and this time it would be the end. But the wave came and we rose to meet it and nothing happened and we pitched forward into the next wave and I could hear it smash against the cabin housing and see the deck beyond the porthole turn white with foam. Then I was out in the cockpit and just in time to see a boat sweep off toward our stern.

It was the big yawl we'd passed on the way out. She must have hit us. I could see the frayed end of her broken mooring line streaming back from her bow. While I stood there, hypnotized, I watched her throw her anchor, skim past our stern and start to disappear into the mist of sea and rain. She had all but gone, when, at the last moment, she began to turn back up toward us. Her anchor was holding. I felt myself relax as I saw her bow take the waves. For the time being, at least, she was safe. I crossed to the other side of the cockpit to survey the damage.

The yawl had rammed a hole in our hull large enough to fit your foot through, but fortunately it was well above the waterline. I found an old shirt in the cabin and stuffed it in. That other noise, from the bow—that was more serious. The cleat must have pulled loose from the deck. Hastily, I crawled up to check it.

You could fit your little finger into the crack in the deck plate, and water was pouring in. The cleat was still there, but the tension was being taken by the rope I'd tied around the mast. I just hoped the mast would hold.

Back in the cabin pumping, I watched the yawl riding the waves behind us, thinking of how lucky it was its anchor had caught, imagining the captain's fear when he felt the rope give and his bow start to sweep around, and how he must have tried to steer her out of the path of the Scatt when he saw her, and had just been unable to do so.

It must have been no more than two hours later when I noticed I was looking beyond the yawl at the surf breaking on Sheep Porcupine. The pump was sucking air, and we were pitching much less, I realized. I dropped the pump and went out into the cockpit. The rain had stopped, and I could see the other boats now, straining at their moorings in the wind. But the wind was down. The hurricane had passed over us and we were safe.

Looking over at the yawl, I saw a figure that was, like myself, standing behind the cabin housing, facing me. He raised his arm and I waved back.

Clint Trowbridge, captain and author

Rev. George A. Trowbridge, father of Clinton

Above: Lucy Trowbridge (left) with a friend of the family
Below: Paul Trowbridge as a young child

Above: Tessa in her teens
Below: Paul at the wheel; Patrick with a cap

Above: Family outing on the Scatt II
Below: The family on board

Above: Scatt II in the New Jersey boatyard where we first saw her
Below: Scatt II at Andrews Boat Yard, Sorrento, Maine
(photo by Sturgis Haskins)

131

Above: The tourist trade, Bar Harbor
Below: Michele aboard the Scatt II off Crow Island

Above: On the rocks off Bean island
Below: Off Brimstone Island

PART THREE

THE CRUISING YEARS

1

The Refurbishing

The tourist season was over, but we had made enough money to have the Scatt rebuilt. When she was finally ready—July 20 rather than June 1 as promised— a friend of ours at the Point asked if he could charter her, and that led to other charters—two for four days each that first summer—which paid the bills.

Fletcher, the boatyard man, had palmed off a Model D Ford engine on me through the mails of winter. A Model D! Could he really have gotten it? Yes, I had his letter. At a hundred dollars, it was a bargain, he had said. He didn't mention the three hundred dollars it was going to cost to get her in the boat and running. The car had been in his aunt's barn for twenty-five years, under a tarpaulin. He remembered riding with his aunt and uncle in the car when the two were still connected, motor and vehicle, that is. In fact, it had been he who had crashed up the car, giving those blessed additional years to that engine, for the uncle hadn't been about to fix it up and Fletcher couldn't afford to. The hundred dollars for the engine would go straight to his aunt, he assured me. That was little enough to do for her in return for the damage he had caused to her car. Thanks to us—him for thinking of it, me for being independent enough to take advice that some people wouldn't have had the gumption to take, just because, on the surface of it...

He'd made the whole thing up, I found out, eventually. But the motor did push us along at more than twice the speed of the old one, and mostly it ran. So, after the chartering caught on, I even found it in my heart to feel grateful to old Fletcher for the con job he had pulled. The day we sailed from Sorrento to Hancock

Point there was a twenty-knot wind and we had the lee deck awash most of the time and SHE DIDN'T LEAK! And then, in between charters, we sailed her, almost every day that it was not lashing rain or blowing a hurricane.

There would be the five of us, along with my parents; Katharine, my younger sister by two years; her husband Phil with whom I'd gone to school and college; their three children (roughly the same ages as our two boys); my nineteen-year-old brother, Gus; and often others, fifteen to twenty in all. It was the ideal boat for such excursions. I knew that already from the tourist business, but it seemed to come to everyone else as a surprise. Lucy and I understood that basically the Scatt was a fine vessel. All she'd ever needed was a bit of refurbishing. But to everyone else, apparently, she was the sinking ship of all sinking ships: born sinking; the only sailing sieve on this or any other coast; a romantic but impossible craft that, like the unwanted house guest, refuses to understand all hints; and stays, and stays, and stays. To them, the Scatt was an embarrassment, I discovered, a further indication, if they needed one, of my mental instability. And all this time I hadn't even guessed at their true thoughts.

One by one, though, they came around. By the end of the summer even my father was grudgingly admitting approval. When we entered the Scatt in the Sorrento handicap and she came in second to last, it was he who said to someone at the Point that she would have done a lot better if what wind there was hadn't shifted around to head her on all but the last course. And when we returned in the afternoon from Bean Island, or Burnt Porcupine or The Hop, and the wind gave out, and I could flick on the engine and stand casually on the wheel box, leaning against the boom, steering with one foot, then I would feel something akin to what I'd experienced during those first trial runs, only now there was something more solid than undampable enthusiasm behind it all. If I'd had to organize a "Save the Scatt Fund," I probably could have done so within the immediate family. But I didn't have to. Even though the bills came to more than we'd expected, the chartering had made up the difference. And now we knew how to finance her for the future.

The Scatt was ours again, and she was practically new. Her eight by eight by thirty foot keel—more putty than wood and broken right through in three places—had been replaced by Maine oak. There were also seventy new ribs, new planking below the waterline, two-inch flooring for the cockpit, a new interior for the cabin; and a new centerboard well made from two-inch cedar that smelled so good it seemed a shame to cover it with paint. It would have been easier to build a new boat, Fletcher assured me. Ironically, painted and in the water, she looked just the way she had when we'd first fixed her. But the lead on her keel was attached by six monster bolts, not just by one.

We didn't have time that first summer for any more extended cruising than an overnight sail with the kids. But the following year we would explore the coast, perhaps as far as New Brunswick. Now that the Scatt was fixed up, she was ready to be taken out of the bay. Even our neighbor in Mantoloking would have agreed. Even Mama Reeves.

2

Roque Island

"Will we make it?" I shout out. The man on the bridge doesn't answer. We are sweeping down on him at about four knots. I have misjudged the strength of the current and am past the aid of the engine's reverse. I can see the man's face now. He's looking down at our approaching mast top with great inscrutability.

"Are we going to hit?" I scream it this time. It's impossible that he does not hear. A dramatic pause. He holds out his arm in front of him, sighting with his hand. And then the shadow of the bridge engulfs us. Smooth water rises in white crests a foot high on the black wooden pilings not a boat's length ahead. We are in the sluice now. All I can do is try to keep the Scatt straight down the middle.

If the top of the mast does not clear the bridge, either the Scatt will come to a grinding and immediate halt, slew around in the current and perhaps tilt over enough to capsize; or, more likely, the forestay will snap like a violin string, or wrench its chain plate out of the bow, and the mast will splinter off at the deck and crash directly onto me. If the mast itself misses me, the whip-like stays will not. Katharine and Lucy, in the cabin, will be all right. Phil is safely in front of the mast on the bow, staring up at the bridge. From this angle it looks certain that we will hit. It's a little like coming down the giant hill of the roller coaster and seeing very clearly that even if you make it to the bottom, there is just not enough room to let you through the black mouth of the tunnel. You sink down in your seat to make yourself smaller and grip the bar in front of you and shut your eyes and scream. You haven't meant to do that, but everyone else is screaming. And suddenly, you're in ecstasy. You scream and scream, at the top of your lungs; and when you make it to the end, you're flushed and excited and you get in line right away to go back up again.

But here you can't scream. The motion is too slow, for one thing, and what would the man on top of the bridge think? It is more like the feeling one has skidding a car on the ice, a sort of slow motion breathlessness. You do what you can; against all instinct you steer into the skid, but you know there's not really much you can do. You'll either hit that telephone pole or you'll miss it. You take an almost detached view of your situation. You hold your breath and, perhaps, at the last moment, you shut your eyes.

The roar of water is in my ears and the bridge itself seems to collapse over us like a circus tent. It is dark and I cannot see.

Suddenly, it is light. I hear a shout from the bow. I look toward the stern, and there is the bridge and the man gazing down at us. We've made it. We're safe!

"Mark it on the chart, will you Phil?" I say. "The fourth log from the top has to show."

"Let's make it the fifth, okay?"

"Okay," I say. Suddenly it is all a great joke, a bit of hokum. I look up gratefully at the solid-looking varnished mast as it cuts through the bluest of blue skies. Jonesport is to our left. Most of the fifty or so houses on Beals Island are down the Reach a bit further on our right.

"That damn bridge," I say to myself, grinning at the memory of what the lobsterman had said earlier that morning when we asked him how much clearance there was.

"Forty, fifty feet. I don't know. Puttin' that bridge from Jonesport to Beals Island is like pavin' a gold brick walk t' the shit house." And it was a toll bridge at that. Fifty cents each way, as expensive as the George Washington Bridge. No wonder most of the people from Beals still went to the mainland in their boats.

"Had a town meeting over to Beals Island ten, twelve years ago," he went on, "about building something or other acrost to great Wass Island so they wouldn't have to wait till the tide was out to slog over in their clamming boots. Well, some of them had in mind a regular causeway, granite blocks and everything, with a paved road acrost the top of it, but there was a considerable number who didn't want nothing. Let 'em wait for the tide the way they always done was their feeling. There were only three families over there anyhow, and no proper road, once you arrived. Even the road on Beals was only gravel. A paved road on top of a causeway would cost as much to build as a town wharf! But there were still a good number of people who wanted something. I'd say the house was about half divided.

"Well, it was a pretty noisy meeting, with a lot of folks getting up and down. Way in the back was Elijah Beal, eighty-two and as lively as a caught flounder. Well, he wasn't being recognized by the chair. He had his arm up and waving but Dave Allen—he was moderator—didn't see him. That's what he said afterwards, anyway. So Elijah just yelled out. He had a good, strong voice and right away people quieted down. You could tell he had a mindfull on him.

"'It ain't no distance 'tween the two a-tall,' Elijah belts out. 'By gorry, I could piss halfway 'crost that gut.'

"'You're out of order,' barks Dave Allen.

"Quick as a whip, Elijah snaps back, 'And if I was in order, I could piss all the way 'crost it.'"

That was the end of the meeting, the lobsterman had told us. And the end of the causeway. It wasn't till last year that they got it through.

"And that was 'cause Elijah 'tweren't there to defeat it."

We are coming up to the dock—just as the rest of the family arrives. If the wind holds, we'll be at Roque by two or three o'clock.

The first time we had come to Roque on the Scatt was the summer before, but that was only for the day. This time we were all going to spend the night. My first trip to Roque was with my parents when I was eleven or twelve and I even remember the way the path that crossed the island looked, as well as the lobsterboat smelling sharply of bait, and the green-and-yellow striped suspenders of the man who took us over. I can see the fan of brown wrinkles that spread from each eye; his short hair, gray, like the deck of his boat; a line of white just above his shirt collar that looked as if someone had pasted it there. He had made us put on musty-smelling, orange life jackets for the trip over from Roque Bluffs. I remember how awkward I felt wearing mine, and how silly I thought it was to have to do so. There was a lot of spray and it didn't take long for my eyes to begin to water as I sat there on top of the cabin roof, just behind the anchor, looking out over the sharp, raised prow, not wanting to miss even a single tree of the approaching land. I had to look back and wipe my eyes every once in a while, furious at the time it took. How could my mother and father sit back there in the cockpit where they could see only what went past them, happily talking to that man? How could they not feel what I found myself trembling with: the sense of discovering a new kingdom?

I feel the excitement build in me again as we approach the end of the thoroughfare and the beach comes into view. No other boats! This is our lucky day.

Roque Island is all the other islands off the Maine coast recreated as one—with the added attraction of a perfect beach from the Caribbean. What is known as Roque is actually a group of islands—Great and Little Spruce, Double Shot, Anguila and Halifax—that extend from west to east for some three miles. Roque itself, which is two miles long, juts to the north of this all-but-linked chain. Its shape—that of a firmly squashed "H"—gives it both a southern and northern harbor. On the chart, Roque Harbor, virtually landlocked by its archipelago, looks something like a giant fetus with the smooth crown of its head and the mile-long beach and its knees tucked up around Lakeman, Bar and Marsh islands—semi-detached peninsulas off the eastern tip. And looking south across this bay from the top of the one hundred and fifty foot cliffs that rise from the eastern end of the beach, it does not seem absurd to think in terms of images of gigantic birth, or to experience this island kingdom as Eden, the Promised Land drenched in milk and honey, a paradise awaiting a golden race. When I came here as a child, what I felt was a Swallows and Amazons sense of adventure and discovery. Now I was with Lieutenant Christian and Ishmael, old Joshua Slocum and Robinson Crusoe, Melville himself. But even more importantly, I was on the Scatt. The Scatt had brought us here. And it would bring us to other places. This was no ordinary boat, but our own staunch ship, a sea-going cruising yacht that held, at the moment, a complement of twelve.

The beach was not the best place to anchor. We would go there now to unload, put the bow of the Scatt right up on the sand, stern anchor set, and form a human chain from cabin to beach, along which would quickly pass all our gear. The others would sleep ashore in three large tents, but Lucy and I would take the Scatt up into Bunker Cove for the night. The previous year's experience had taught us that.

Thud! Thud! Again that dead sandbag jolt just beneath my bunk. Black night in the cabin. Outside I could hear a gale blowing. The Scatt was being driven onto the beach, I finally realized. The anchor must have dragged. Instantly, I was outside in my pajamas, fumbling with the motor. The bilge was relatively dry, I noticed, as I opened the hinged aftersection of the motor hatch and found the shut-off valve with my flashlight. Thud! It was right under me. Fortunately, the anchor was still keeping our nose into the wind.

I pressed the starter for the third time. At last the motor sputtered into life and I shoved her into forward. One more terrible thud and then we were off—pitching into three-foot waves and just barely making headway, but free, away from the beach; safe. Lucy took the wheel while I stumbled up and got the anchor in. There was an eerie, predawn light in the direction of the wind and we motored slowly but steadily out into it and toward the thorofare, the narrow gut that separated Roque from Great Spruce—for the virtually complete protection of Bunker Cove.

No. I would not try to anchor off the beach again, even though I had seen other boats do it. It was too risky. Anyway, Bunker Cove was the coziest anchorage on the coast. When we'd finally gotten there that previous summer—after a good hour and a half of slogging into freezing, rain-filled wind—we sat tight in the only really good spot and watched two other boats flounder and scramble for something that would hold them. There was a deep maroon Herreshoff cutter of about forty feet that lurched herself over the pilings of an old fishing weir across the thorofare from us in Patten Cove, though without damage, apparently. The other boat—a thirty-five foot ketch that motored up from where it had anchored off the beach—finally tied a bowline to a tree on Little Spruce Island after repeated failures to get an anchor fast in the current of the thorofare. No, Lucy and I would head for Bunker Cove as soon as we'd all had dinner and while it was still light.

We were just about to go when I heard cries from shore, and saw arms waving me in. It looked like Dunkirk: everyone down by the water, extra clothes and sleeping bags held high.

"Sand fleas! Millions of them. As large as cockroaches. In my sleeping bag!" Peter says hysterically. "Each one with real pinchers that BITE!" Well, what could we do? I have motored the Scatt back into the beach and we commence with the Exodus, leaving the tents

143

and camping gear where they are. Twelve people sleeping on the Scatt! Twelve people just being on the Scatt is crowded enough, but sleeping! Just finding a place to lie down is going to be a major problem. It's too dark to find another good spot. We'll have to anchor off the beach.

Fortunately, there are no mosquitoes. I wrap the end of the flying backstay around my sleeping bag at the knees and secure it to the cleat, thus giving myself a better chance of not falling overboard in the night. My shoulders are in the widest section of the deck, back by the stern where the cockpit coaming circles over to the wheel. Even so, my right shoulder presses up against the wood, while my left sticks just over the inch-high outer rail. I am lying down, however; fully, if uncomfortably, stretched out. That is more than Phil is. He lies huddled in a fetal position on the four-by-three-foot engine hatch. Lucy has a place in the cabin, but I do not exactly envy her. Paul and Patrick are burrowed in blankets at her head and feet. Tessa lies on an air mattress on the floor six feet away, and Katharine and her three occupy the other ten-foot bunk. Jean, the youngest, is a nice, quiet three year old, but still... The two boys will probably end up on the floor. It is crowded and it will undoubtedly be noisy in the cabin but at least they've gotten rid of Phil, who had planned to sleep on the floor just under the ice chest and storage cabinets, his feet dangling back into where the motor is housed and the bilge. Phil snores, like the proverbial man cutting wood. So now I have him, three feet away. I roomed with him at college so we can share the outer darkness and the night, my sister reasons. Gus is out here, too. He has made a sort of hammock out of the sail and is lying in that. Good luck, Gus.

Phil and I talk for a while and then I hear the rasping sound of a wood file and know that it is just a matter of time until the trees start coming down. I lie there on the hard deck strangely happy. Venus casts her silvery path across the bay at our feet. She is so bright she seems like a sibling to her fair cousin the moon. More stars emerge. There is a light breeze from the sea which keeps the mosquitoes away and stirs tiny wavelets that make soft music with the hull. Muffled noises from inside the cabin rise to an occasional cry, a reprimand, a plea. Tomorrow we will have races on the beach. We will climb the cliffs again and stare out over the bay, the magic circle of spruce-fringed islands and the pure, white mile-long crescent of sand. We will have a gargantuan grilling of hamburgers and hot dogs at noon, and some of us will dip into the mild surf and pretend it is warm enough. In the late afternoon, we will pack up our tents and slowly steal away so that everyone else will be able to get back to Hancock Point by evening. Lucy and I and Katharine and Phil will find a cozy anchorage for the night and take a leisurely three days to make the return voyage. We know now about the bridge.

Phil has settled down into his bucksaw-kindling stage. Things are quieting down below; the drone of the bees is distant. I count shooting stars until my eyes will stay open no longer. Thoughts drift in and then out of my mind, pleasantly, like mist in a valley, and then I fall asleep.

3

Some Bridgework

As a concession to our former way of life, every once in a while I would take out a group of tourists on the Scatt. I couldn't do it the old way, at so much a head, because of the Coast Guard; but I could charter the boat with captain, by the day, at a fixed price and let the groups form themselves. One such was Camp Wissopee, from Bridgton, four hours away. A platoon of girls would drive over for a long weekend, camp in and around the Scatt, which I'd moored off an island a mile away up Skillings River, and mornings I'd take out one half, afternoons the other.

One time, in order to acquaint the girls with the open sea, we sailed half the camp over to Bar Harbor during the morning while the others drove around in station wagons. The wind was strong and puffy and I'd taken in a reef before exchanging groups at the municipal pier. What I should have done was cancel the afternoon sail and refunded their money, but that's an observation made in retrospect. At the time, the reef-taking seemed an eminently sensible, perhaps overly cautious, maneuver. We took a puff, washed the lee deck, the girls screamed; and in the brief lull before the Scatt rocked back onto an even keel, the mast broke. It was undramatic but definite. I heard something splinter and my eyes fell on a wedge of wood sticking out from the mast an inch or so. When I brought the Scatt up into the wind, the mast closed up again, but the stays were so slack that I had to tie them together with ropes. We motored into Bar Harbor for an early end to the trip; and for the next three weeks, until the mast was spliced and back in the boat again, we motored around barge-like, bow archly raised and mastless, the castrato of sailboats. What we did mainly was go under bridges.

If you're going to explore your kingdom in a sailboat, either every bridge has to draw or you've got to do your cricking in the dinghy. Without the mast, the Scatt could get anyplace a canoe could, practically, and so we set about it. We glided up the almost slack water of Tidal Falls, ducked under the bridge at West Sullivan and spent a leisurely three hours exploring the all but empty shores of Hog Bay. A mammoth granite pier was evidence of West Sullivan as a port in the coastal schooner trade, and we marveled at the thought of sailing ships five times our size coasting up the narrow river to load granite or lumber here in the deep water on the other side of the bridge, then falling back on the ebb to Sullivan Harbor, Frenchman Bay and the sea. Puttering around in Hog Bay we, ourselves, delayed too long. The falls were roaring when we returned.

What held us up was our debate as to whether to try to make it through the tidal creek that goes under Route 1 and creates an island out of Hancock Point for a few hours every day. After much conversation and crude measurement, we had finally given up the glorious thought of circumnavigating Hancock Point in the Scatt and were moving down toward the bridge more or less in defeat, when we began to feel the pull of the current. Little eddies, foam-flecked whirlpools, encircled us. Off in the distance we could see the white water of the falls and hear its roar. Theoretically, there was no problem; there was ten feet of water at low tide. All you had to do was steer to the left of the rock that was in the middle of the channel. The current would sweep you there anyway. In actuality, though, being sucked into that mill race at an ever-increasing speed was something very different. The tide ripped through here at twenty to thirty miles per hour, and for one hundred yards or so the whole area was a cauldron of foam. The waters of Hog Bay cried for release. The tidal plug had been pulled and this was the drain. On paper it wasn't dangerous, but if you got caught in this sluice there was no going back.

"Throw the anchor," I cried as we swept down toward the bridge.

By the time Gus had the anchor ready, though, we were through the bridge, mostly sideways; and I gunned the motor to give us steerage, told him to forget it and aimed us for the left of the channel. There was a minute of panic and then it was like going down the shoot at the fun house. We bounced along on our big red bottom, slewing this way and that, and all too soon spun out into the flat water below the falls and the ride was over. If we could have gone back up and done it again, we would have. What a ride!

A few days later, on a dead high tide, we tried to get up through the culvert that tunneled under the road at the end of Partridge Cove and almost got ourselves corked in. We went up every tidal creek and under every bridge in the area; and then, because we'd been frustrated before in the attempt, we chugged the forty miles to Addison and went under the bridge there and seven miles up the Pleasant River to Columbia Falls.

Ever since the second summer of the refurbished Scatt—when we'd gotten them to open the bridge for us over the Machias River so we could sail up to Route 1 and have strawberry pie at Helen's Restaurant, going through drawbridges on the Scatt had become something of a craze. Some of the bridges, like the one at Addison, had to be arranged in advance. That was the pity of it, that it was a complicated maneuver taking several days; and up to the crucial point it had gone off without a hitch. The day had been fair, the seas calm. The tide was just right. We'd even arrived when we said we would. And there they were: three bare-backed men pushing at what looked like a subway turnstile while the ancient drawbridge creaked and groaned but did not open. There was quite a crowd gathered—twenty or thirty people, and the mood was distinctly in our favor. The man we'd called had informed us the bridge hadn't functioned as long as he'd been in charge, fifteen years, but he would try it. What a cry went up when they broke her free and a section of the road that was the bridge began to angle off parallel to the river. There was even a certain amount of traffic held up, though most of the cars had come for the event. Finally, when the turntable was at ninety degrees and the men were resting on the six-foot wooden spikes, we were signaled forward. The passage was narrow—no more than ten feet to either side—and the current was with us at about two knots. We motored sedately toward the opening. Kids on their bicycles stopped. The crowd was breathless. All eyes were trained on us. All but one pair, that is.

"She won't clear the wire!" We looked up at the hill on our left where the ominous voice had come from, and then we saw it too, a single swaybacked strand suspended between two poles that would snare the mast by about six feet if we kept going. With great churning of waters and groans on all sides, I put the engine into reverse and slowly we backed away from success. It was no good. The party was over before the champagne had even been uncorked. There was nothing that could be done about the wire, so back we went, back the forty miles to Hancock Point—a four-day trip in all.

Going under the bridge at Addison without the mast in her and with only a few people around to watch was something of an anticlimax, but at least we had the satisfaction of evening up the score. But when we'd done that, there was nothing much left. As a motorboat, the Scatt had certain advantages; but they were all used up now, we felt, and we yearned for the new mast with increasing ardor as the last days of August flashed by. When it was finally ready—too late for that summer—it brought with it an additional note of gloom. The bill was four hundred and thirty-five dollars, almost twice the estimate. I'd gotten a teaching assistantship for the coming year. I would be working three-quarters of the time while I finished up my degree. And that four hundred and thirty-five dollars, I figured out in a moment of severe depression, represented just about one-eighth of my new salary.

4

The Summer of the Summer Camps

It was the next summer, the summer of the summer camps, as I don't like to think of it. Inspired by my success with Camp Wissopee, I had written letters of advertisement over the winter to some fifty camps. The response, though hardly overwhelming, was sufficiently large so that by the end of August I never wanted to see another child again between the ages of ten and fourteen, at least not in any sort of group.

And then there was the ignominy of that day late in August. No, I shan't forget that. And I do blame it as much as I can on the camps. If I hadn't been feeling so harassed, so battered, so beleaguered by the kids, it never would have happened. That's what I like to tell myself.

I hate looking at charts. I like studying them. I adore to pore over a chart trying to visualize what a certain anchorage looks like, grinning at or pondering over the names of reefs, coves, islands, bays (Egypt Bay? Money Ledge? Burying Island?). I love to study the bottom, trying to picture that weedy world of hills and valleys: life as a crustacean, the weightless soaring of fish. But I hate having to constantly consult a chart, particularly if it's of an area that is, presumably, utterly familiar to me. Like the waters off Bean Island, for instance, a mile east of the dock at Hancock Point.

Try drawing a sketch of the back of your hand without looking. You are sure you can, until you try it. If I could paint, and someone commissioned a series of pictures of Bean Island, drawn from memory—ones that would take it all in, even from the air—I would cackle with pleasure at the ease of the assignment. I could go on for pages describing Bean Island. I'd camped and picnicked on it so many times that familiarity had all but bred contempt. Unless there was no wind at all, we never went there anymore. Too many other people used it. It was flat and tame. There were no cliffs to climb, no ocean swells to watch and listen to, no caves of dripping kelp to explore. And the waters around the island were all too familiar. At least that's what I had always thought.

I don't know how I could have made such a mistake. In broad daylight, fifty feet southwest of a black nun four hundred and fifty yards off the northwest tip of Bean Island, with great thoroughness and perfect placement, I, Clinton Trowbridge, a sailor and navigator of some presumed accomplishment, on a falling tide about half an hour gone, put the Scatt up on a ledge. Almost instantly she began to list to starboard. I didn't float her off until ten-thirty that night. And by then everyone who owned a camera in both Hancock Point and Sorrento, and some from as far away as West Gouldsboro and Lamoine, I understand, had a magnificent shot of the entire port side of the Scatt. It was a perfect day for camera work. I'd even placed her right as far as the sun was concerned. My brother-in-law was so delighted with the results of the pictures he took that he sent me a whole roll, the two best frames enlarged. She was beautifully exposed, all right, the soft blush of her underbelly naked to the general view. The Scatt on parade. Entertainment for the whole community. People I didn't even know would smile at me and mention it at the post office, outside the church, in line at the Ellsworth movie theater. If that's what being a celebrity is like, I don't want it. Not ever again. Once was enough. Why didn't I have the presence of mind to charge admission? Because I was too bebothered to think straight.

I'd always thought of crashing up on the rocks as a particularly horrendous form of mutilation. Actually, if it's done properly, it can be quite pleasant. There we are, sailing along as peacefully as you can be with twelve howling demons aboard, when I hear what sounds like a pile of stacked cobblestones collapsing and feel a motion that is somewhere between road testing a car without shock absorbers over a stream bed, and waterskiing. Simultaneously, there is the sharp report of something going off below. As soon as we have grated to a halt, leaning over on the kickstand as if to say "We have arrived!," I look into the cabin expecting geysers only to see the centerboard sticking up through the middle of the table. The three-quarter-inch oak pin on which it pivots, I discovered later, broke when the centerboard reefed out. There seems to be no other damage. The kids from Camp Wissopee, back for more adventures, are, of course, delighted. They pile over the sides, clothes on and everything, and we are too busy keeping tabs on them to even think about getting the Scatt off the rocks until it is much too late. By one, stuff is already starting to fall about in the cabin. We have ascended the ledges by at least one vertical foot, I estimate. I hope the next high tide will be a full one and that it is enough to float us. I wouldn't want to wait for the equinox. I pile things on the lower bunk and contemplate rescue. When I emerge from the cabin, I see the counselor had already out-thought me and is rowing a group to Bean Island, where the other half of the campers are conveniently stationed already. In half an hour I am alone. The captain does not desert his ship, I tell them, feigning sorrow at the parting. By the time the Scatt is fully exposed, the first of the boats arrives.

From one-thirty to six it is picture-taking time. They circle like gleeful sharks, coming in close for the kill. I go below and try to ignore them by reading a book, but usually someone calls and I must show myself and exchange pleasantries; and then my brother-in-law arrives. He has red hair and laughs a lot, and he is laughing now. Howling with laughter. But he has brought some beer and sandwiches and is planning to stay and help me get the Scatt off, so gradually I forgive him. He even gets me to stand next to the bow in an attitude of mock pride. The white hunter and the blue Hippo that gave him such a fight. All bye-bye now. Isn't she a big one, though? All very amusing. We float the Scatt off without incident. So there is a happy ending.

The next day, the last for this last of groups, praise God, we side-slip around the bay doing a good deal of motoring to windward; and two days after that I take the Scatt to the yard for the winter. We have only one more week before we must leave anyway, and I want to get the Scatt off my hands before anything else happens to her. Rehanging the centerboard is a relatively easy job, but I am going to let them do it at their leisure after she is out and it is even easier. I keep thinking of how I would have felt if I'd really bashed her up. What if the bow had hit head on and slid not so nicely up over? What if a boulder had blasted through her hull, or a knife-edged rock pierced her side as she'd settled over on the ledge? I had felt her spine-like keel sway, could imagine her ribs springing, then settling back again, as she climbed that underwater precipice. What if her keel had cracked, or broken in two, or in three, as it had before we'd bought her?

So I take her to the yard early. Better let well enough alone. We've made some money, enough for a new sail and anchor line. More importantly, I have snared a job teaching English and will be dragging down the magnificent sum of five thousand dollars this coming year, none of which is for the Scatt. My first full-time job!

5

A Journey Through the Hebrides

The most perfect times of all were when Lucy and I could get off by ourselves. There was one cruise in particular, on the way back from Roque, that stands out: our first long trip with the new sail.

The new sail was a disaster in one sense, a great success in another. It was much easier to handle. I could now sail the Scatt by myself. The trouble was that it looked so awful, and it was harder than ever to go to windward. The new sail was Marconi rigged. By mistake—a triangle replaced a lopsided square. We stored the gaff.

The hundred-year-old man who'd made it for us in Jonesport for one hundred dollars had become confused. When I'd brought him the old sail to copy, I'd wondered aloud how a Marconi rig would work, and apparently he took that as an order. But then what he used was his wife's sewing machine, and where he did the work was the kitchen, so I suppose it's a miracle he got anything right at all. Anyway, the Scatt was safer as well as easier to handle with about a quarter less canvas to catch the wind, and after we got used to how ridiculous it looked, we liked it better than the old one. Not my father and not my brother—they were all for having it re-cut. But the rest of us. We were more practical.

The waters east of Mount Desert have fewer cruisers in them and there is a more rugged untamed sense of beauty about the coastline. Prospect Harbor, Cape Split, Jonesport, Machiasport, Cutler, Eastport; these are fishing villages. The silhouettes of cruising boats do not disturb the lobster fleets. Everything that the coast of Maine has, there is more of eastward: fog, rocks, islands and tide. As you approach the Bay of Fundy, the tides double and redouble in size and force. From Roque on you sail with them or not at all. The Reversing Falls at St. John make those at Sullivan look like ripples in a creek, but they are as nothing to the great tidal bore encountered further east. The Bay of Fundy is shaped like an open-ended bathtub and functions in the same way. The waters slosh as much as seventy feet up the mud banks at the very end, pushed from the other side of the Atlantic. From Schoodic Point east, the people seem almost a different breed. Well before you get to Canada, you have the feeling of being in another land. A stretch of roughly sixty miles as the cormorant flies, this easternmost tip of the United States is our Hebrides. These are the real cruising grounds.

It was the first time we'd sailed by ourselves in these waters. We left the others in the late afternoon at Roque Bluffs after almost a week of family cruising. So, being suddenly and happily alone was all the more enjoyable.

We spent that night at Bunker Cove with our favorite seagull. I don't know how long gulls live, but this one we'd known for three years and he was handsome and old and imperious then—the point of a wedge of lesser gulls that paddled behind him in disorderly and uneasy ranks. We were having dinner in the cockpit: lobsters, what else? We were right off the cliff, just inside the osprey nest that partially obscures the view of the thorofare, and Lucy was throwing pieces of stale hamburger bun to the gull. He was more like a dog than a bird, a well-behaved Labrador who gets the scraps before they hit the floor but who stays a non-barking, non-slobbering, respectful distance from the groaning board. The other gulls would flutter around above him, diving in recklessly every few minutes, but his footwork was faster than their wings. He was probably five yards off our stern, but never once did he fly. He moved with the precision and speed of a lobster boat jockeying up to a float, could turn on a dime; and only once did another gull get in ahead of him, and that was when two pieces came at him too close together. He was the king of blackbacks, and the white of his head and his massive chest shone like ermine. His back and sides glistened as if freshly anointed. His gray eyes gimletted us both, and the spot of red under the curve of his yellow beak was the richest of jewels.

Bunker Cove is where an American privateer hid successfully from the British during the War of 1812 by cutting down the masts of his ship and strewing its decks with the limbs of spruce trees. Lying at anchor, surrounded by the forest primeval, it was easy to imagine the scene: the British rowing uneasily through the thorofare, fearing ambush, ill at ease anyway in this strange and forbidding country, a sentry peering out from the hulk, perhaps, or from the protection of a wall of spruce.

A blue heron flew up the cove to where it showed mud. It began to get dark, and after the gulls left, the quiet was so absolute that you hardly breathed. The next day was warm and sunny, and we lolled on the beach until noon and then sailed with the wind to Head Harbor and The Cows Yard, another, even more completely inland-like sea pond southwest of Roque by three or four miles. To be in a boat surrounded by water that is, in turn, surrounded by land not much more than a stone's-throw distance in any direction is one of the coziest feelings there is. It's like the womb, I suppose. And if the wind howls outside, it is even better. Or if there is fog.

We woke the next morning to a wet, gray blanket. The wind had shifted to southwest in the night. I had smelt it at dawn when I'd come up on deck—the smell of the sea. Billows of moisture blew in through the neck of water that connected us to Head Harbor. You could hear everything, see nothing.

Shortly before ten, a lobsterman materialized, hauled his trap practically out from under our bow, and was about to disappear again into nothingness when I called over to him. Yes, we could follow him out, if we liked, behind Steele Harbor Island and into Eastern Bay. Mud Hole Channel was clear. We could sail out past Great Wass Island and perhaps get as far as Corea by evening, which would bring us to within an easy day of Hancock Point. But wait a minute. On the chart, the channel was so narrow it was only a line of blue and most of it was marked two feet. I was just trying to figure out what the tide was now when he threw me a line. It would be easier if he towed us. So off we went at full gallop, so close to the ledges off Crow Point that we must have ridden over them on our bow wave. There was a stretch of open water through which we stampeded, and then off our left bow—the compass needle hadn't varied since we'd started—was a black buoy: Calf Island. The fog was still thick so he led us to the channel and pointed us toward the sea. We motored blind for half an hour at 140 degrees and then we turned west. A breeze would come up before long, he'd assured us.

By noon we were ambling off downwind, and before the afternoon was over, we were planing down the sides of four-foot waves. Squinting into the dying sun, we sailed into the tiny harbor of Corea. Sailed! There was barely room for the boats to turn, they were moored so close to each other. And when we dropped the anchor, we saw we were the only sailboat in the fleet. The fog came in again during the night, but what did we care? It gave us an excuse to spend another day there. And what a day it turned out to be, at least for me.

6

Encounter in the Fog

We should have realized immediately that he was not all there, but we didn't. We were sitting in the cabin, tied up to the fish wharf in Corea, trying to keep dry and warm, when a big moon face appeared in the doorway. He looked friendly, and the first thing he said was, "You want some beans?" And then he offered us two, quart-sized mason jars. That got him in the door. He sat down on the step, a large, shapeless man in his forties, I guessed, with blue denim overalls and jacket; boots, and a new-looking green cap that was a trifle large for his head, peak slightly askew. He just seemed to want to talk. Perhaps he lived by himself and was lonely, I thought, trying to imagine what his life was like.

He asked us a lot of questions about the boat, and then, out of the blue, he said to me, "Come on. We row out—get some crabs." With a look at Lucy which tried to say, "It's okay. Don't worry about it. Couldn't we use some crabs?" I let him lead me out to the deck and our tiny dinghy.

"Where to?" I said, and he pointed just off my left shoulder into the dense fog and somewhat too excitedly, I thought, whispered, "Got a whole crate full of good crabs." We were surrounded by fog. Beads of moisture formed on my upper lip. My eyebrows were heavy with dampness. If I hadn't taken notice of the current, I wouldn't have had any idea of how to get back. He kept pointing, though, and I continued to row. The white hull of a lobsterboat would take on form, and I would clatter an oar against its side. Or I would smell the bait as we glided by, invisible, shrouded in a damp, though penetrable, gauze. Sure enough, in a few minutes we came to a mooring with a crate tied to it. I reached over to pull it aboard, but he held my arm.

"What'll you give me for 'em, eh? What'll you give me?" He was leering at me in what seemed a pretty blatant way, and I noticed for the first time how black and ill-spaced his teeth were and how powerful-looking and large his hands. He had small, blue eyes, and the rims around them were red; and there were flecks of spittle at the corners of his mouth, and his lips were unusually full and soft.

"What do you mean?" I said, my voice sounding strange and high to my ears.

"Want you should give me something," he said. "You know what, I bet." And he leaned forward till his face almost touched my own.

"What? What is it you want?" I mumbled, nervous as hell now, wondering what I might have said that would have led him on like this.

"You can marry people. What you said. A captain of a ship could marry people." That's right. I had said that, joking about the prerogatives of the seafarer's life, back there in the cabin. It was shortly after that that he had suggested this trip. What did he want me to do, marry him? To whom? Or was this some sort of "let's play doctor" game, the rules of which I hadn't yet understood?

"You can marry and bury and do all things like that. What you said." He was laughing in a crazy sort of way, cackling would be a better word. His head was bobbing up and down, and his right hand felt heavy and very solid on my knee. Should I try to reason with him, or just strike out at that childlike face and hope to knock him overboard? Probably he couldn't swim. Most natives couldn't. With those boots on he wouldn't be able to get far anyway. If I waited much longer he would be the one to make the move, that much seemed clear.

All at once he stopped laughing and grabbed me by the shoulders. There was an intensity in his face that

I could not meet with my eyes. What he wanted, he would have to have. There would be no refusing it. I waited for him to come closer, for his breath to touch my face. "Baptize me," he said. "You got to baptize me. I'll give you all those crabs. Every one."

I almost laughed aloud realizing that he simply meant what he said and that my going on about the extraordinary powers of ships' captains had led him to think I was some sort of priest. Should I just baptize him and let it go at that? Why wasn't he already baptized? Perhaps he'd been going around for years like the Ancient Mariner, trying to get himself baptized and nobody would do it. Were there, perhaps, legal complications, obligations, if a layman performed this rite so jealously guarded by the clergy? Perhaps a voice would boom out of the fog, lightning would strike, a whirlwind would gather...

"I can't baptize you," I said to him.

His eyes became dull, and he hunched down in his seat like a dog that's been whipped. To make matters worse, he forced the crabs on me anyway, all of them. I told him that captains could marry people, but they weren't allowed to baptize. Only a priest could do that. There was somebody in Ellsworth, or surely Bangor, who would be happy to do it, I assured him. He didn't seem to be listening, though. When I told Lucy about it later, she said I should have just gone ahead and baptized him. Some part of me has always regretted that I didn't.

7

The Great All-Night Sail to Roque

The story has gotten so completely out of hand now that it has virtually reached the proportion of myth: the all-night sail to Roque in the fog with the half keg of beer left over from my father's sixty-fifth birthday party, with a captain and first mate who were as desperate a twosome as you'd be likely to run up against this side of the Yukon. The trip was saved, if not redeemed, by the crew, and the cargo was the undamaged but untransformed object of beer-soaked, besotted brigandage. The voyage itself was an odyssey of such bathetic proportions that in the chronicles of absurdity it is assured a certain niche. Every time we see Henry, our black Episcopal minister friend from Charleston, South Carolina, which is about once a year, he tells an even more exaggerated version of the night's events than the year before. It is time to set the record straight.

Henry and his wife, Owilinder, Phil and Katharine, and Lucy and I were sitting around in the living room about to run out of conversational steam and totter off to bed, when Phil, who has an abiding fascination for what he calls The Big Idea, suggested it. An all-night sail to Roque, picking up the troops in Jonesport in the morning for a day on the beach. The summer was nearing its end. Last year it was Katahdin or bust; a twenty-four hour round trip—three hundred miles, not counting the climb. The summer was two days longer as a result. That was reason enough for doing such things. Phil and I would go—now, of course. There was no time to lose—and who else? The four boys. That was Phil's idea, too. They were late enough in their prepubescence to be able to relieve us at the helm, and it would be an experience they would never forget. A trip with Dad. At the very least something to write compositions about when they got back to school. Who knows? A rite of passage, perhaps. When we got everything ready, we would carry them down to the boat in their bedclothes and stow them aboard. No need for elaborate explanations. Let them sleep on, until two or three in the morning. By then we would be well out beyond the islands and into the open sea where we could set a compass course—due east—and safely turn things over to them.

I drew another pitcher of beer and came back into the living room. I suppose it was the sight of that great vat of spirits that gave me the idea. "We'll throw the keg on, too," I said. "We can sell it off mug by mug in exchange for lobsters," I added, thinking of all the times we had bartered that way with fishermen in the towns that were dry. We had the charts out by this time and were showing Henry and his wife what the thirty miles of coastline looked like. There were no shifting sandbars to worry about. It looked harder than it was because of all those islands and rocks and reefs. Actually, you just went straight south until you could clear Schoodic Point, and then you turned east, and by the time you were at Libby Light it would be morning. All those islands and coves were a great security. If a big wind came up, they offered protection, something that wasn't so easily available along the southern coast off which they fished.

"So how'll you be able to see at night?" Henry asked.

"Oh, there's always light enough for that," I assured him, and Phil nodded. "Anyway, there's a moon." We went outside to look at it.

"Brrrr!" shivered Henry. "Doesn't it ever get to be summer up here?"

"Henry," I said, "you're coming with us."

"Oh no you don't. You don't catch me..."

"Go on, Henry," said Owilinder. "You'll enjoy it."

"Grab him, Phil," I said.

So the Reverend Henry Grant was shanghaied. Okay, that much I admit. But if you wanted to get technical, so were the boys, and they didn't think of calling it by a dirty name like that.

Henry's leather soles slipped on the rocks that paved the terrace. I had him under the arms; Phil had his knees. Once we got him into the dinghy, there was no going back. We left him blustering on the Scatt while we rowed ashore for the rest of the ship's company. He pleaded. We were merciless. No, we didn't bind his wrists and ankles with ropes and gag him with his own handkerchief. He'd made that part up. He could have swum ashore if he'd wanted to.

Midnight. We were motoring along the Point into a light sea breeze. If the wind held like this, we'd be able to sail to Roque on a long reach, I said. No motor noise. Just the gurgling of beer and the lapping of waves. The seven against Roque, heroes all. It was a perfect night. The Scatt was a vessel tried and true, and we knew the waters from here to there like the proverbial backs of our hands.

We greeted the first mishap with howls of laughter. That is, Phil and I did. Henry let out a cry of despair that suggested the Book of Lamentations. For the umpteenth time we had been showing him where we were on the chart—just passing between Burnt and Sheep Porcupine islands—when lo and behold, the freshening breeze caught the chart and whisked it overboard. Whoops! Oh, well. Only a few more miles to go on that one, anyway. We tried to get Henry to see the merriment. The chart was "gone with the wind." Ha! Ha! No response. Nothing.

The second unfortunate incident rather severely limited our options, but it wasn't the doomsday that Henry saw it as. Simply fog, thick enough so that we couldn't take a chance on sailing back through the islands into the bay—not without a chart, anyway. You couldn't see the bow of the boat, as a matter of fact. Still, we were in the open ocean and the breeze, which had picked up considerably, would really push us along when we made our turn, in an hour or so.

"You mean we're going to sail in this?" cries Henry, in utter disbelief.

"It's safer than trying to get back," I tell him matter-of-factly.

"Safer!" he cried. "I don't want any part of 'safer.' What I want is 'safe!'" He goes below. He really is angry and scared now, and that bothers me, but only slightly. For one thing, I am getting very sleepy, and for another, I am still up to about my navel in beer. The voyage continues to be propelled onward by the force of The Big Idea, but somewhat less strongly now that it is cold and wet and two in the morning and the Scatt is pitching so uncomfortably in the waves. Phil brings out some coffee from the cabin, and Henry, who is heavily bundled up now as if for the arctic, joins us again.

"If I'm going to die, I want to see it coming," he moans.

All four boys are still asleep. I ask Phil to take the wheel for a while. I really cannot keep my eyes open.

It is smelly and uncomfortable below, but I fall asleep immediately anyway. I am awakened almost at once, it seems, by the sound of the motor going off. Phil and Henry are struggling with the sail. The boys are up too. We are pitching worse than ever, and sloshing from side to side as well. Groggily, I lurch out into the cockpit just in time to see Henry almost decapitated by the boom. "Turn the engine back on," I yell. No one else knows anything at all about sailing. Phil has always been hopelessly disinterested in the thing itself, only in what the thing brings; and Henry, we have discovered only recently, has never been on a sailboat before.

I get the engine running and the Scatt headed back into the wind. Phil handles the sail. Up she goes, backstay tightened, centerboard down. Now we can turn the motor off. Right away the motion is more comfortable, just like a big rocking horse. I can hear Henry sighing with relief, his hour not yet come. I get us pointed east, and then I turn the wheel over to Paul and suggest that he and Philip take the first watch. They can trade off and at the same time keep each other company. Paul's face is serious and white in the dim glare of the flashlight. Philip is huddled in the deck chair, a sleeping bag enveloping him like a cocoon. It is a little past three o'clock. At four-thirty they can turn things over to Peter and Patrick, and at six, if they must, they can wake either Phil or me. Paul has just turned twelve and is the best sailor of the group. Philip is four months younger. Patrick and Peter are both ten. All have sailed some in the White Seal.

"You mean you're going to go to sleep again?" says Henry.

"Sure," I answer. "We're all set now."

"I'm staying right here," he grunts. "Right up here so I can see what's going on."

The fog is just as thick as it was before, but I don't make an issue out of it. I just say okay and head off for the sack. Phil does the same.

"We could hit something," cries Henry. "Something could hit us. What if there's another crazy boat out here? What if...?"

"If you hear a foghorn, wake me up," I say. "No chance of hitting anything else out here."

Before I go to sleep this time, I have mild pangs of remorse for having dragged Henry off on this trip. I can see the boys aren't too happy about it either. They don't seem as excited as we thought they would be. If I'd known Henry had never even been out of the harbor in that boat of his... I snuggle further down in my sleeping bag, head buried beneath a cushion, in a vain attempt to keep out the sounds of Phil's snoring. He's lost his spark, too, I notice. I hear him groan in his sleep and shout out. I think about the first time he and I sailed to

Roque at night, in that tin boat we chartered in Camden the year before we both got married. We were with Katharine, Lucy, and Paul Van Dyke, a sailing buddy we picked up at Seal Harbor because we knew he'd want to come—and besides, we were a little nervous about making this first trip by ourselves. Good old Paul, with his sea boots and pea jacket and his two six-packs of beer. He'd sailed us there practically by himself, while we slept below. What a beautiful night that had been, too. Moon almost full, gentle following wind, practically no sea at all.

And then I thought of the other time, three years ago, sailing up here with my father and Gus and his fiancee, Marty, in a chartered boat because the Scatt was out of commission, briefly; and I felt the muscles in my calves tense up, and the pressure pass up along my back and cramp my shoulders. I turned over onto my left side and tried to push the image out of my mind, but it wouldn't.

Not till I'd gone through the whole thing and felt the sweat wet against my face on the canvas seatcover beneath my cheek, not till then did the vision pass and let me drift off, one ear cocked as it were, for the wind's howl.

We'd motored all night. Both Lucy and I had been seasick, something that very rarely happens to either of us. It was just past dawn, maybe five o'clock when Gus woke me up to take my watch. We were about five miles outside of the Brothers, heading for Roque. It was mostly the relief of finally being able to sail, I guess, that caused me not to pay the right kind of attention, but when the wind suddenly came up strong out of the northeast, all I could think of was to get the sails as trim as possible. It turned out to be a line squall. Black clouds like shaggy eyebrows hooded Jonesport. Then the whole sky turned black and the sea looked as if it had suddenly been whipped up by a gigantic eggbeater: there were three-to-five-foot waves, all of them cresting. Everything started to fall inside the cabin, and then there was the screech of ripping canvas, and the jib and jigger were flapping loose and useless. I let the mainsail down into the sea, had the motor on and was turning up into the wind, before my father, his face a chalky white, appeared. It all happened that fast; there were no more than a couple of minutes from the first breath of wind to this. Getting that jib in was horrendous, I'll never forget the bowsprit plunging me all but under each time we came down into the trough of a wave. It was all I could do just to hold on. When a particularly strong gust hit, the bow slewed off to the right and the raised hull caught the wind. Only her heavy keel saved us from capsizing then. The Scatt would have gone over, for sure. Certainly her engine would never have brought her back up into that wind.

Henry is pounding on my shoulder and shouting into my ear. "A ship! We're going to be hit!" I hear the foghorn myself now. It is ear-shattering and seems to be right in front of us. I rush on deck and bring the Scatt about, praying I am not turning into the path of this behemoth.

"My God, a waterfall!" shouts Henry.

Breakers! Off our stern. And then I realize what it is and my relief is so great I all but laugh out loud. What we hear is not a ship but the diaphone on Petit Manan. If I'd turned the other way we'd be on these lighthouse rocks. Ten minutes I'll give it before we head downwind again, and then there really is nothing in our way until we get off Great Wass Island and the passage into Jonesport. Already the sound of the diaphone is less harsh, less terrifying.

"A waterfall in the middle of the ocean. Oh my God, if I ever live through this night," Henry wails like a prophet. "Lord save us and deliver us. Good Lord, protect thy servant. Protect thy people."

I am wide awake now and stay at the wheel when we make the turn eastward once more. Paul and Philip are already asleep down below.

"Come on, Henry," I call out, trying to make my voice sound cheerful as well as reassuring. "There're no waterfalls in the ocean. You know that."

He doesn't answer, only moans on and on.

It is still dense fog at seven o'clock and quite dark, but I'm sure I know where we are, so I head us off to the northeast in hopes of hearing the diaphone on Moose Peak. I think I've heard it already, but I cannot be sure. In ten more minutes I do hear it, and I show Henry where we are on the chart. Henry's eyes have red rims around them, but he looks more forlorn than frightened. And tired. He looks as if he could sleep for a week.

"Mistake Island," he growls out. "Indeed it was." But I can tell by the lift in his voice that he's forgiven me the worst part of it, that he already has plans for how he will celebrate the end of this nightmare. His spirits rise even more with the lifting of the fog and the warm sun and the sight of Jonesport in the distance.

"Mudhole Channel. Mistake Harbor. Nats Rock. The Nipple. Not even Nipple Island, just Nipple. My God. And will you look at it? It's a nipple, all right." He starts to laugh, quietly at first, then louder. "A sweet, ever-loving woman's nipple on a beautiful smooth breast, and it looks like you didn't kill me after all unless you put us up on one of these rocks, and if you do that, I'll just get off and walk to Jonesville or whatever crazy place this is; and if you think for a minute that you're ever going to get me out here in any kind of boat again, you've got another think coming, because if I'd known then what I know now, I would have held on to something back there or jumped into the sea like Jonah at the very beginning, or knocked you both unconscious with a stick or a wrench or something and taken command of this ship myself."

Phil and I are exhausted and too relieved to be in Jonesport to listen much to what Henry is saying. Also, the jubilant tone of his voice grates now a little. The boys are asleep and I am very hungry all of a sudden.

In broad daylight the Scatt looks terrible and smells worse. The aluminum beer keg squatting there in the cockpit reflects the sunlight into my eyes. It has been dribbling and drooling all night and the floor is like flypaper. What will Henry really say about all this?, I wonder. What will the boys tell their mothers?

Phil has cooked oatmeal and made coffee. That makes us feel a lot better, almost human, in fact. We get to the dock at nine-thirty and everyone is there already, waiting to be taken out to Roque.

"Henry," Owilinder says, "my Lord, you look like a ghost."

"And that's almost what I was," Henry yells up at her, "traveling around with this crazy fool here."

Owilinder tries not to laugh but cannot control herself.

"You've turned two shades lighter," she bubbles out. "White as a sheet. Oh, Lord."

Everyone else is laughing now, too. It's true, Henry looks as white as I do, whiter in fact, for I am burnt black by the sun.

"What a mess. You all look terrible, and look at the Scatt!" Lucy says. Some local fishermen gather around in an amused group as we haul the empty beer keg up the side of the wharf with the detached halyard and then roll it over to the car. It will be crowded enough aboard the boat without that. We throw water onto the floor, but what it needs is a good scrubbing.

We motor up the Reach toward Roque. Everyone else is looking forward to a day on the beach after a good night's sleep. Henry should be more tired than anyone, but apparently he isn't anymore. He tells the story over about ten times and already there are embellishments. Later on in the day, as I try to sleep, lying on my stomach on the warm sand, I can hear the laughter build up and burst out and die down and build again, and I can just imagine the new horrors he's invented.

Half of me wants to get up and defend myself, but the other half won't move; so I lie there until Patrick runs over and starts to trample on my back with his bare feet.

It is only in his most recent retelling of the story that the waterfalls have gotten back into the account.

"Like Niagara, I swear to you. And the ship that came at us out of the night, it stood there like a cathedral. It towered, an immensity, like the sheer cliffs of a mountain. I tell you..."

"Henry! There was no ship. That was a lighthouse. Petit Manan Light. Those were waves breaking on the rocks."

"And those children, those innocent children, in the cold and the dark, shivering, uncomplaining, standing up to their terrible and frightening ordeal like the martyrs of old. While their fathers slept! Do you hear me? Their fathers snored away in their beds, mindful of nothing save the comfort of their own loathsome bodies, slept like..."

I try to interrupt, to still this terrible voice, but Henry pays no attention. He is making a performance out of this nowadays, getting his licks in, I suppose, for my kidnapping him like that and almost killing him. That's why it's important to get all this down in black and white. The sober correction of truth, so all will understand what really happened.

8

The Discovery

We had been moving north over the years. Now we were in Long Island, close enough to Maine to think seriously about sailing the Scatt down at the end of the summer. Our house was near the water. We could keep the Scatt in all winter and save the yard fees. I had romantic visions of excursions around Manhattan, explorations of Gardiner's Island and the outer bays, shark fishing tournaments off Montauk, trolling for blues in the Sound. Why limit the Scatt's use to two months when you could sail her year-round? For the real winter—December, January, February—I might put in a heater and rent her out to some hard-up college students. Or we could sail to Florida over the mid-semester break. Start her down in short hauls over a couple of long weekends in November. Maybe get her as far as Charleston before Christmas. Then we'd have January to make it the rest of the way. Or the Bahamas. Why not go there instead? Two days out into the Gulf Stream, and then real summer: the baking warmth of the tropics—bonito, millions of desert islands to claim as our own. It was ridiculous to limit oneself just to Maine.

It was August 10th. We were going west again, retracing our steps, only this time the Scatt was in good shape. For crew we had Patrick, our husky teenager, and Frodo, the ship's mascot, a long-haired dog of mixed origin, mostly German Shepherd and wolf. Two years before, we'd lucked into a twenty horsepower Gray Marine engine, built some time in the early thirties but very little used. Under power, the Scatt's cruising speed was a mighty six knots. The party at the dock was sorry to see us go—no more sailing picnics for that summer, or mad excursions into the night—but they would not be entirely boatless. The previous summer, Gus and Phil had gone in together on a lobsterboat, a real lobsterboat from Jonesport that steered with a stick and had that characteristic high and mighty bow. They'd fixed her up with deck chairs and a good marine motor, an automatic bilge pump that worked off two batteries and many other items. They went out separately or together, and with their more powerful engine, it was nothing for them to go to Turtle Island, twelve miles away, for the day, or into Blue Hill Bay.

"Goodbye, goodbye!" Waves of hands. It was hot and muggy, a good day to be on the water, even though there was no wind. We stopped at Northeast Harbor for the night, and the next morning exchanged a few words with Bobby Kennedy, who sailed out past our stern in a fifty-foot varnished-hull sloop.

"Where are you bound?" I called out.

"Roque Island," he replied, his attention on the spinnaker.

"A good spot," I yelled back, purely for effect.

We were headed for McGlatherey's, off Stonington, an island paradise we'd been camping on for several years. The water was warmer than at Roque, and there were usually fewer cruisers, though once an entire boys' camp descended as we were setting up our tents. McGlatherey's was owned by The Friends of Nature, a group founded for the preservation of such places. We had actually grown to like it better than Roque, though there was a certain tameness.

The last time we'd been near Roque was to look at some islands that were for sale. Over the last few years we'd looked at dozens of islands, miles of shore property. The Hancock Point house was bursting at the seams. There was need to expand. It was a frustrating search; the islands had impassably rocky shores or mud or were too expensive or too remote. One island in particular that seemed ideal from the shore turned out to be a jungle of felled trunks in a marsh when we pierced its veneer. Another had no trees at all and no place where you could land a boat. The Ram Islands, though, were perfect: papa, mama and baby Ram—fifteen acres in all, only a mile from the general store on Beals Island, and far enough into the bay for us to feel protected. We walked over them and around them and through them, planning empires. But we were too late. They had already been sold.

From Northeast Harbor to McGlatherey's was only eighteen miles, but all day we tacked into a mild northwest wind, so by the time we got there it was late. We dropped anchor anyway, even though there were two other boats in the harbor. The next morning we got an early start, and because the wind was still northwest, we decided to shoot for Matinicus. We'd never been there before and it seemed the perfect time. You picked your day to go to Matinicus if you were in a small boat. It's a real sea island, ten miles off the tip of Vinalhaven. For us, a twenty-mile reach out past Brimstone and into the long swells of the real ocean—those modulations of the deep: the sea's slow breathing. It was always a little scary sailing in the open sea.

Patrick loved it. He would sit or stand at the end of the boom, bouncing along as if on water skis. Or he would climb to the crosstrees—hand over hand up the halyard, using the masthoops as toe holds—and stand there for hours. It made Lucy nervous, but there was no stopping him.

At four o'clock we ducked along the lee of No Man's Island, and in a few minutes we were moored in Matinicus Harbor. Few cruisers or anyone else came out here. There was a shyness you didn't encounter in other places, the timidity of the closely related and the ancient born. There were no summer houses, no accommodations for outsiders. The general store was the most complete I'd ever seen, the wild roses and hollyhocks surely the brightest. It was for the clarity of the water in the harbor, though, that I reserved my extra portion of awe. We could literally read a newspaper that was spread out twelve feet below us on the bottom. It was almost dizzying, this floating on nothingness. We seemed anchored in air.

The next day we tacked till late afternoon, ending in a tiny deep-water harbor between Andrews and Camp islands, in the Dix Island group, ten miles to the northwest. There were cellar holes all over Andrews Island, the remains of some hundred houses. The island had been quarried for its granite during the early nineteen hundreds. Pink-flecked or gray, this smooth-grained granite was Maine's gold for a while; the islands its Klondike. Now there was only one house in the whole group, a camp set up by some summering lobstermen from Rockland. Why hadn't we thought of trying to buy one of these?

Friendship, two days later, was busy and industrial, the brackish waters foul. There were houses on all the islands and a bevy of small boats. We welcomed the swells that crashed on Pemaquid Point as we rounded it a day later in a smart sou-wester, but Christmas Cove was a disappointment. Not only was it a solid deck of mahogany, but even empty it would have been nothing special: a nice place spoiled by too many houses.

The Damariscotta River, though. What a toboggan ride! We kept the reef we'd put in the day before but even that proved to be too much as the williwaws descended. Going dead before the wind, there was the constant threat of jibing. It was Patrick who thought of using bed sheets instead. The Scatt would do about three miles an hour on her hull alone. With one sheet tied to the running backstays and the other bellying out in front of the mast like a spinnaker, we became a clipper ship and skimmed along at six knots. A square-rigger at last. I hardly had to touch the wheel. And the river itself— with its rolling farmland interspersed with forest of hardwood, and its coves and promontories—had a comfortable, uncluttered, settled look. We celebrated the beginning of our second week of cruising at a wharfside restaurant that evening in Damariscotta, the three of us burning with the heat in the unfamiliar enclosure of a building.

Two days later we were in Boothbay. I had remembered Boothbay Harbor as a pleasant, though touristy, town, something like Bar Harbor but on a smaller scale. It was more like Atlantic City: everything jammed up and blaring. We didn't even go ashore, just circled for gas. We'd motored in about three, but by the time we'd worked ourselves up to the gas pumps it was an unbelievable four-thirty and we were in the foulest of humors. Every stinkpot ahead of us seemed to have depthless tanks and a marvelous capacity for oil. They were motor cruisers, Mafia boats, we called them, particularly the Big Daddies, the destroyer types with shark-like bows and two sets of portholes—air-conditioned aftersections of zippered canvas. After we filled our tanks, we were in such a hurry to leave, we didn't remember that Frodo, the beautifully shipbroken, had been neglected since early morning. Instead of going back (another hour in line?) we stopped outside the harbor beside a small island and Patrick rowed Frodo ashore. Jockeying to keep out of the path of the fleet, Lucy and I weren't aware of what had happened until Patrick reappeared alongside in the dinghy. "He tried to shoot him," he shouted. "A man came down with a gun and pointed it right at Frodo, and if I..."

"He did what?" I asked.

"And there were two huge dogs. This man came up to me..."

"Did Frodo get a chance to...?" Lucy asked.

"He shook the gun in my face. He said that he was sick and tired of chasing dogs off his land and the next time he was just going to shoot."

"Did Frodo go?"

We both looked at her. She didn't seem to understand.

"Frodo's right here," I said.

"No. I don't think so. Maybe," said Patrick, laughing.

It broke the tension. We all laughed, briefly. And suddenly we were determined to go no further west. If it was this bad in Boothbay, what must it be like in Mamaroneck? I remembered, as a matter of fact, what it was like in a lot of those places. I remembered also the sense of arrival we'd felt once we'd passed the Cape Cod Canal.

What were we doing going back into all that? Were we crazy? Did we think that what we thought of as Maine was every place? And what made us imagine we would be as free the rest of the year as we were now? We hardly needed to discuss it. We took Frodo ashore near the Coast Guard station on otherwise deserted Burnt Island, and then we let the sail out and headed east. It would be downwind all the way home.

9

Crow Island

I give myself the credit for it, but as a matter of fact, it belongs to all of us, or none. Maybe it should be given to Frodo. Or the man with the gun. The way I argue is that if I hadn't been nice enough to do the laundry that afternoon, it never would have happened; and that's probably true but perhaps unimportant. What happened was that on my way back with the bags of wash, I passed a real estate office and, mostly to rest my weary feet and partly out of habit, I went in and said to the lady there, "Excuse me. I know it's a stupid question and it's probably been asked of you a thousand times already this summer, but by any chance do you have any islands for sale?"

There was a short pause. Then, very politely, she said, "Why, yes. One of them is more of a point. It doesn't have a name. The other is Crow Island. I have two pictures of it." She'd received the listings the day before. I looked at them on the chart she opened up for me and there was no question in my mind which was the best. The other island was way up in a muddy bay where the mosquitoes would kill you even in August. Crow Island was a mile off Sunshine, on the east side of Deer Isle, halfway between the Reach and Merchant's Row. The pictures were small but in color. We were headed that way anyway. We would look at it and call her: the Shepard Real Estate Agency in Stonington. I will always feel like one of her lambs.

Patrick likes to give himself the credit, for he argues that without his insistence that we should rule out nothing, I would never even have asked. Granted, I had crossed out the whole area as too beautiful, but that was not because I felt unworthy. I just figured it was hopeless, that there would never be any islands for sale around here; and if, by some miracle there were, the price would place it out of sight. I had asked only because the years had hardened me into an asking machine on the subject. "Excuse me. I know it's a stupid question, but..."

Lucy tends to side with Patrick. The thought was the all-important thing. We were ready for something like this. What we'd been really doing all along was island hunting, not sailing to Long Island. But if anybody deserved the credit, it was the Scatt, she said. She had taken us there. Without her... Okay. We were in the right place at the right time with the right attitude.

In spite of the dead trees that gave it a scraggy look from a distance, right away we loved it; there were seven or eight acres, mostly field. Approaching it from the south, we could see the land rise gently in the direction of Sunshine to some twenty or thirty feet. She lay east and west, a lopsided oval with a ledge attached to her northwestern tip. The southern shore had little to recommend it for swimming—a boulder-strewn beach with a useless crescent of white sand at the top—but it was entirely composed of pink granite. Crow Island shimmered there before us in the afternoon sun—flesh-colored, infinitely inviting. Then we rounded the western tip and our breathing quickened as we saw the sandbar that ran out to the smooth pinkish rocks of the ledge beyond. It was low tide, yet from the looks of it, the beach extended out in both directions as far into the water as one would ever care to walk. There was a line of sturdy-looking young trees hugging the shore on our right. Then, as we rounded the ledge, we saw a shallow harbor—perfect protection from anything but the northeast: a crescent of boulder-dotted pink sand beach about one hundred yards long. Beyond that, on the eastern tip, were smooth ledges of coral-colored stone backed by a clump of ancient spruces, a couple of giant birch trees and a jungle of raspberry bushes.

We landed at the harbor beach, climbed the steep twelve-foot bank up to a field of rustling grass and stood looking out at Mount Desert Island eight miles or so to our north. Then we turned to where Isle au Haut rose purple in the south, a hopscotch of islands in between. "We could put the house here," Lucy said. Two fifty-foot spruces framed for us the thousand-foot peaks of Acadia National Park. The opposite view would be of islands and the open sea.

We went ashore at Sunshine and called Mrs. Shepard. Yes, we could leave a check there with the Heansslers. She would pick it up on her way home. There was a party that had just driven in from Vermont coming out to see Crow in the morning, but yes, she would tell them it was sold. After we'd gotten to Hancock Point the day after tomorrow, we could call her and work out the details. The hundred dollars was not refundable, of course. We understood that.

"Yes! Yes! Yes!" I could hardly contain myself. I had no idea how we were going to finance it. All we knew was that Crow Island was ours.

* * *

We almost didn't get it. We had no money, so we had to go in on it with people who did: Katharine and Phil. We called them from Bass Harbor that night and they met us in the morning. Even then Philip almost fouled us up with a girlfriend he was visiting on one of the Cranberries. He had to be picked up, and that would delay us. For how long? Blah, blah, blah. Finally, I had to become theatrical. There were millionaires from Vermont hovering over the shores probing for any signs of weakness, etc. etc.

When she first saw it, Katharine was visibly unimpressed by the silhouette of Crow's dead trees in the distance. She gave me that "You brought us all the way

180

here for this" look, but we fed her mind with future delicacies; and when we did get there, it was only a matter of minutes before they too were helpless under the spell.

We worked out the financing at Union Trust in Ellsworth: a ten-year mortgage, and my part of the money down in a short-term loan. We had the closing on the 28th of August. The previous owners (a brother and sister who had been counselors at the French Camp on Deer Isle but who had since moved to California) had sold it to us at an eleven hundred percent profit after owning it for three years. But three days after the closing, we were offered three times what we paid for it. And the next year there were no more islands. We'd bought it just in time.

10

The Zonker

What with building a house on Crow, the Scatt got very little of our attention that next summer. Living on an island, too, was a continuous cruise: the world flowed past without end and we, the shoreline, were the fixed point. Oh, we still went sailing, but it wasn't the same.

Even though it was only a one-room octagon, the expense of building made me all the more reluctant to finance the Scatt. I thought I wouldn't put her in at all that summer, but the family rebelled. They loved the all-day sails to neighboring islands, the cranberry picking and the fun of exploring at close hand what the horizon only suggested in patterns of color and lines of form. I, too. But another boat would have done as well for these excursions; better, in fact. The Scatt was slow. It was a three-day expedition around Isle au Haut; about the same to circle Deer Isle. We didn't go cruising anymore. We had so much else to do. Five days, round trip, to Hancock Point for a visit was our only venture out of the bay. And then we acquired a beaten-up Boston Whaler and the Scatt was shoved further into the background.

The whaler was jutting out of one of the sheds in the boatyard, half full of water. As soon as I found out it belonged to the fifty-foot English yawl that was being fitted out to go around the world, I knew it would be for sale. They couldn't very well tow that. For sixty dollars it became ours. Another two hundred dollars got us a secondhand twenty-five horsepower Johnson outboard. Until then our island launch had been a ten-foot dinghy powered by a constantly failing three-point nine-horse

Mercury. Now we had a real boat, christened the Zonker. Before the first week was over we'd gone around Isle au Haut (eight hours) and circumnavigated Deer Isle as well (ten). We could make Hancock Point in an hour and twenty minutes through the Narrows. Our world was suddenly extended. It was as if we'd been living in slow motion before.

The Scatt's motor was on the blink that summer, so when we went out on family excursions, we towed the Zonker; and if the wind failed, we pushed her home with that. But we only went out perhaps a dozen times. The Scatt didn't sail well with such a hulk in tow. Paul and Patrick took her out for three days with some friends, but we worried the whole time because they had no power; and when they got back, the sail was ripped badly enough so that it couldn't be patched just by us this time. We could take it to the sailmakers, but what we really needed was a new one. A new sail, and a new motor (or at least a valve job). The Scatt was getting old again, but now we did not really need her. It was time to think of selling.

But to sell her you had to have her in good shape. It was a vicious circle. So, against the advice of the boatyard, we ordered the valve job done. (They would have scrapped the engine.) Success! For a mere two-hundred and forty-eight dollars we now had a circa 1930, twenty horsepower, Gray Marine engine in running order. A re-cut, new-looking secondhand canvas sail set us back another two hundred dollars. We painted everything, including the motor, and by the time the ads came out, she looked so good we could hardly bear the thought of even showing her.

We were just admiring the way the new sail set and how nice and white it was, when I brought the Scatt around on the port tack and we heard the familiar sound of splintering wood. Sure enough, there was a fault in the varnish running right along the line of the old splice, and this time it wasn't repairable. Fifty dollars worth of long distance phone calls and I still couldn't find anything in the way of a secondhand mast. A new one cost fifteen hundred dollars and even if we'd had the money, we couldn't have had one made before the middle of August. Just so we'd have something, Paul and I stepped a sixteen-foot log that had been cast up on the beach the previous winter. We scouted out two thirty-foot poles and made a lateen rig, tacking a triangle from the old sail onto the poles with roofing nails. Amazingly, it worked pretty well. It was quite a job hauling her up, and we didn't even try to go to windward; but this way at least we were able to use her. Actually, we used the Scatt more that summer than the one before. But, of course, nobody bought her. Nobody even looked at her, in fact, once we told them about the mast. Another boat sailed up to us one day in August, though, and told us how great we looked, and we liked that. Perhaps this was the Scatt's ultimate rig; her declining years would be spent as an Egyptian dhow. A romantic idea, but the reality was that we had to find her a new mast, and at nowhere near the new mast's price.

We searched and called and inquired, and finally we settled on aluminum and not a mast at all, but a flagpole—a hollow aluminum flagpole manufactured by The American Flagpole Company of Setauket, New York, a mile and a half from where we lived. The aluminum was a quarter-inch thick, and no one, including Mr. Billings at the boatyard, had any doubts about its being strong enough. Unconventional, yes, but it would definitely serve. And the price, delivered, was just under seven hundred dollars.

11

Adrift

It was barely light, but I had not slept because of the storm. Forehead pressed to the cold glass, I strained to see through the sheets of rain. She wasn't there. The Scatt was gone; she had broken loose or dragged her mooring. She must be on the beach. The rain blew halfway across the room, hissing on the blackened coals of the fireplace. When I opened the door, Lucy stirred. There was no sound at all from our youngest, sixteen-year-old Michele.

But the Scatt wasn't on the beach. The beach was a wreckage of seaweed and driftwood, great white combers bursting onto the rocks, sending spray up as far as where I was crouched, behind the big spruce at the top of the bank. Hunched over against the driving rain, I ran back toward the house and down the path that led to the sandbar. She wasn't there, either. The tide was high, going out. She must have missed the island entirely, sailing on her hull across the sandbar. She'd be on the ledges south of Sunshine somewhere, I said to myself mechanically as I ran along the edge of the bluffs, wondering when she'd broken free.

And then I saw her, sailing along at an angle to the wind, heading for Conary Point, a good half-mile south of Sunshine. I must have left the centerboard down, I realized, noticing how well she was pointing. There was some time then, perhaps enough to get to her before she hit. If only I had the Zonker. But the Zonker was at the wharf in Sunshine with a broken drive shaft. I'd have to go in the dinghy. I ran back to the house to tell Lucy. She wouldn't want me to go, but there wasn't time to argue or explain. The waves were a good six feet high, the crests blowing off into sheets of spray in the leveling wind. I'd have to take each one like a surfer. That was all right. I'd done that before, plenty of times. It was almost the end of August and the water was comparatively warm. Even if we went over, I'd make it to shore.

The motor buzzed off at the second pull, and then we were careening down the side of a wave that half broke over the stern and I was in the bow, banging at the handle of the Mercury with an oar to keep her on course, and bailing when I got the chance. Buried in the troughs or huddled down to avoid the stinging spray when we hung on the crest, I could see virtually nothing. I inched us south, seeking the island's lee. Then I would be able to get my bearings. If only I still had the extension pole, I thought, as we swerved dangerously off to the side; but that had been lost in a storm ages ago and never replaced, for normally we only used the dinghy to get to the Zonker or to tow behind the Scatt.

What I couldn't believe was the speed. I'd been thrown out of an MG once, doing sixty miles per hour on a curve. I remember only the sensations of the first few seconds. Then I was crawling out of a weed-choked ditch, numb and feeling strangely detached, as if my body were another, smaller vehicle in which I also traveled. It was a little like that. Only so far we hadn't turned over. Not quite. And then, suddenly, we weren't going so fast anymore. The whole process of steering became easier. I could almost relax.

I raised my head and through the rain I could see the western shore of Crow Island a quarter of a mile away. The waves were a mere three feet, the wind something you could at least look into. I lunged into the stern seat, and as I turned to face the bow, I saw the Scatt not half a mile away, still sailing in the direction of Conary Point. I was going to get to her in time after all. A wave lapped over the stern and I shifted back to my seat in the bow. Our lee was gone, but we had come halfway, I figured.

Perched at the crest of a wave, I caught a glimpse of the Scatt. She was as far away as ever, it seemed, but now it looked as if she would be blown past Conary Point, toward the reefs this side of Little Lazy Gut Island a half mile away. I had hoped, I realized, that somehow she was going to sail into Conary Harbor, berth herself miraculously at the lobster dock there, and all I would have to do was jump aboard and tie her down.

"So now you have more time," a voice said. Another fifteen minutes before she crashes up on the rocks or comes to her end on the ledges of Little Lazy Gut.

Earlier that summer I'd awakened in the night, stood in the field and watched the Scatt drifting off up the bay. The wind had come from the opposite direction then and hadn't been as strong as now, yet the Scatt had pulled her mooring. Something had warned me and I had awakened Patrick, and we had gone out together in the dinghy and gotten to the Scatt without much difficulty, and brought her back in. How I wished Patrick were with me now.

Over the years there had been so many instances of near disaster that part of me could not imagine a final catastrophe. There was the time Lucy and I had been caught in that fierce wind off Jonesport, when all the mast hoops broke at once, suddenly, with the noise of a half-ton Venetian blind crashing to the ground. We'd thrown the anchor, but even with all the scope out it hadn't held; and we'd drifted down onto an island, and then, unaccountably, around it, until the anchor had dug in at last. Two old men had rowed out from the shore half a mile away in a peapod, just to tell us not to worry, that the Coast Guard was on its way.

I was behind Seal Rocks now, and the seas were calmer. For the first time I could see the Scatt clearly. She was about a quarter of a mile away, sailing sedately but swiftly along on her hull. Directly in her path was a ledge. I could not hope to get to her in time.

As I came closer, I saw her turn abruptly, then lean over on her side and right herself once more. I held my breath, waiting for her mast to topple, for the waves to crash over her as she began to break up. But nothing happened. She simply remained where she was—tilted at a very slight angle, a line of waves beating against her stern, but not all that hard. The ledge she had chosen was a smooth one, and she had hit it just right, apparently, for she was resting at the top of it, perched there, half out of the water, having slid into a sort of cradle at the ledge's peak. As I circled around behind, I came under the lee of her bow. Her hull was unscarred. She had done it again! All I would have to do was wait for the tide.

The centerboard had plowed up into her trunk with such force that it had raised the table top half an inch. But there was no other damage. Even the rudder was unharmed. And that evening the wind went down; and when the tide floated the Scatt around six o'clock, all I had to do was turn on the engine and motor her back to the mooring.

12

The Last Sail

Paul and Patrick had started out early Wednesday morning and were at the mouth of the Benjamin River by eight-thirty. They'd had a week of bad weather, and even though twenty to twenty-five knot winds were predicted from the southwest, October 24 was late in the season and they wanted to get the Scatt put up for the winter, wanted the responsibility off their backs. Getting to Billings boatyard in Stonington meant they'd have to take a long tack around Crow Island, but that was all right. They had the whole day for it.

At first everything went well. All the way to White Island they roared along on a reach. But then the trouble started. They probably should have put in a reef, Paul said, but they wanted to make speed. Also, what with the work they were doing on the old farmhouse we had bought in Sedgwick, they hadn't been out on the Scatt in a month and they were enjoying themselves, having fun. Then they picked up a lobster pot rope just as they started heading up toward Crow, and by the time they'd freed it from the rudder, they could make only the middle of Swan's Island. The wind was really blowing now, and they hadn't realized the tide would be against them, so by the time they crossed the six miles over to Swan's Island, they could barely make Buckle Island at the northern tip. And then the real trouble started.

Paul had been telling me all this on the phone, and I was already having visions of disaster just from the way he was talking. I'd seen him rattled only about three times in his life, and here he was barely able to get out the story and obviously understating it like crazy. And then I realized today was Thursday, the 25th, which meant it had taken them two days to get the Scatt to Stonington.

"So is the Scatt all right?" I asked, more or less breathlessly. There was a longish pause.

"We made it. But not by much."

Numbed, I couldn't respond right away. Finally, I grunted out something or other, but by then he had continued with the story. All I could do was listen. By this time the wind was a good thirty-five miles per hour. Practically every wave was spraying back over them in the cockpit, and the steering kept slipping. The cogs would jump off the track and the Scatt would come up into the wind, and half the time when she came back down again she'd be dead in the water. Paul would have to let the boom out into the trough to spill the wind and then pull it in slowly till he got up enough speed to haul her way in again. By this time Patrick was bailing pretty steadily straight from the cabin into the cockpit. Every time they seemed to be making progress, a squall would hit, and try as Paul would, he couldn't keep the cogs from tripping, and the Scatt would veer up into the wind and the whole process would be repeated. It was exhausting, and the worst thing was that they weren't getting anywhere. And then, right off Buckle Island, a particularly vicious squall hit and the mainsheet parted; and by the time they managed to haul the boom back in, they were on the rocks.

I couldn't believe what I was hearing. It was as if I was there with them but they couldn't hear me. Why hadn't they lowered the sail and turned on the motor? Why hadn't they reefed? If they were that close to shore, why hadn't they thrown out the anchor? Why? Why? Why?

As if anticipating what I was going to say, Paul explained that the motor hadn't worked, that they'd also lost his dinghy just about then and in slewing around looking for that, had picked up a bunch of lobster pot lines. Then, when the mainsheet had parted, Patrick had had to shinny halfway out on the boom to get the frayed end of the line; and by the time they'd reeved through the new one, they were on the rocks. They hadn't realized the ledges stuck out so far.

"But you got the Scatt in," I said.

"That was the miracle part," he said and gave a little grunt of a laugh.

They heard the centerboard hit, and Patrick jumped off the bow. Even though the keel had already hit once, he was able to push up the bow on the next wave, and instead of crashing down onto the rocks and staying there, the Scatt slid to the right. He jumped back on, got out the anchor, threw it and then got the sail down, and the Scatt leveled off with her nose into the wind. There were rocks all around, but the ones in front of them gave a tiny bit of lee.

"Boy," I said and laughed to myself in exhaustion and relief.

They bailed for awhile and she didn't seem to be leaking too badly, so they checked out the motor and all it was was a loose wire. She started right up. So the worst part was over. They motor-sailed her back across to Sunshine—with two reefs in—and Paul's girlfriend, Jennifer, who'd been looking for them in Stonington, picked them up in Sunshine. The next day, today, they'd motored the Scatt around to Stonington in a dead calm and turned her over to Billings.

"Pretty hairy," I said.

"I guess prob'ly," said Paul.

Struggling with the boom, they must have looked up and seen nothing but breaking seas all around them. And then they'd hit. And they had no dinghy. And they were a mile from land. And what would they have done if the Scatt hadn't slipped off but had broken up on them, had bashed herself to nothing on the rocks? It wouldn't have taken long. And this time of year the water was freezing. And they were already exhausted. There would have been something left for them to stand on, to cling to, at least; but how long would they have survived among those ledges? Would they have been able to last out the night?

I blamed myself, in large part. There was a list a mile long of things that needed fixing on the Scatt that I hadn't gotten around to. I had bought the Scatt a new mainsheet just before we left that summer. I'd noticed that one of the strands on the old one had parted. I'd gone right out and bought a three-quarter-inch nylon line, but what with one thing and another, I hadn't put it on. Had I done so, I realized, the near shipwreck might not have occurred. Had I checked out the engine more faithfully, or done a dozen other things, perhaps none of what happened would have happened. On the other hand, if Paul and Patrick had been in less of a hurry, had waited a day, had checked the engine before leaving the mooring, had themselves reeved on the new mainsheet before taking off... No, I would feel thankful instead of guilty, and glory for the umpteenth time in the fact that apparently the Scatt always knew better than we did anyway—that given half a chance she would slip past the rocks, and would nuzzle her way into safety.

* * *

The next year we didn't put the Scatt into the water at all. We'd owned her for twenty-five years. She'd brought up our children and my sister's and my brother's children, too. She'd brought us all up—and out and into and away from. Without the Scatt, we would never have found Crow Island. And without Crow Island, Paul wouldn't be living in Maine now—in Sedgwick, at the mouth of the Benjamin River—and might not even be married to Jennifer, whom he'd met while working at the Jordan Pond House on Mount Desert Island three summers before. Without the Scatt, Paul and Patrick would never have learned how to sail. Paul would never have bought the White Seal, the family sloop I had learned to sail on as a boy, would never have fixed her up and chartered her out and finally sold her when he got too busy with the house he and Jennifer were building in the woods at the top of a hill in Sedgwick. Without the Scatt, none of these things would have happened. But the Scatt herself had had her day. Even after we got the new mast, we hadn't been using her. That was the other thing. She had become a mere pleasure boat, and we all had too much to do and too many other places to put our money. And every year she cost more. It was costing us a hundred dollars for each day we sailed her that last summer, and that was ridiculous. So once again we put her up for sale, and this time we meant it.

"Ten thousand dollars. She's worth at least that much," I said.

Lucy shook her head, and the rest of the family agreed. But I wasn't going to let her go for nothing. I put her in the Maine Coast Fisherman without response, tried to sell her to the Mystic Seaport Museum—they had enough "classic" sailboats, especially catboats, and I brought the price down several times. Finally, in the spring of that year, 1979, a man from Connecticut went up to Billings boatyard in Stonington to take a look at her. When he returned home, he called me up furious. "What do you mean by advertising that wreck for sale? She's hogged out. There's no canvas on her cabin top. The motor's obviously no good. I didn't even find the gaff... "

"Just a minute," I said. "What do you mean 'hogged out'?"

"Her stern's dropped. She obviously needs to be entirely rebuilt. I wasted two days and..." There were no other calls.

When we got up that summer to look at her, it was true. She looked terrible, worse than when we'd first seen her in Mantoloking a quarter of a century ago. The canvas that covered her cabin had indeed ripped, and I stripped the rotten rest of it away with a pull of the hand. Inside, she was a mass of peeling paint and water-stained boards. You could see daylight through some of her seams, caulking was sticking out in several places, and there was, I had to admit, a slight sag to her. Mr. Billings was a bit more optimistic than the man from Connecticut, but not much.

"I don't know about 'hogged out'! Seems to me her lines have kind of slipped, but that could be a couple of things. Could be she just needs refastening. Have to give her a good looking over to tell much, take off the garboards, anyway."

Taking off the garboards, not to mention "anyway," would cost about half of what we were already paying just to leave her there for the year in her cradle, which was a lot. And what would we do about it when we found out what was wrong? "Thirty-four foot cat-boat, built in 1928, rebuilt 1954, hogged out 1979. Marconi rigged (accidentally), leaks badly above and below, motor no good, no anchor (someone had stolen it), new mainsheet. Seven thousand dollars (crossed out) $5,200. Call..."

There were a whole slew of old boats in the back part of Billings boatyard. Great hulks rotting away. That's where the Scatt would end up in a couple of years if we did nothing. The graveyard. But what could we do? We did our best to ignore the problem all that summer.

We'd brought a ridiculous little boat up with us from Long Island—a tiny, flat-bottomed but very heavy sailing skiff nine feet long with an absurdly awkward and badly fitting gaff-rigged sail—and we sailed on that some, but without great enthusiasm. Everyone felt the loss of the Scatt. It put a pall over everything. Leaving her there to rot to death at Billings was like abandoning a member of the family—a venerable and beloved aunt or uncle or grandparent. Not quite, of course, but hogged out or not, almost certainly no one would want to buy her in this condition. Could we justify offering her for sale at any price without spelling out the whole awful truth? There seemed to be no good solution. We left her at Billings for the second straight winter, feeling guilty and depressed and trapped.

13

Mr. Scott to the Rescue

Putting the Scatt up for sale at two thousand dollars, I justified as a gift. The lead on the keel alone was worth half that. The new mast, the mainsheet... But underneath, I felt like a crook. Whoever bought her was in for a pack of trouble. In July of the following summer, we got our first inquiry—a phone call from California. I answered all Mr. Scott's questions with a certain degree of ambiguity. Yes, she did leak some, but really no more than most older wooden boats in her condition. The cabin definitely needed to be recanvassed. Not a huge job really (if you butted up against the hatches and the trim). Mr. Scott was a hard man to discourage, however, even if you were being terribly clever. "We'll be coming next week," he said. "My wife and I."

"What if you don't like her?" I couldn't help but blurt out.

"Oh, we'll like her, I'm sure."

As it happened, he came by himself. He rented a car at the airport and was walking around the Scatt with an uncontrollable smile on his face when I met him at Billings boatyard. He was a stocky, red-faced, white-haired, very jovial-looking man who I guessed was somewhere in his early sixties.

"Plenty of room in her," he said. "I'll take her."

"But don't you want to see the sail and...?"

"We can do that later," he said. "Let's go back to my motel so that we can close the deal."

We got to his motel room in Stonington, and I made him out a bill of sale. I was waiting for him to pull out a check when he said, "Excuse me for a moment," and disappeared into the bathroom. Before I had time to ponder the matter, he returned carrying a stack of bills and what turned out to be a money belt. He proceeded to count out twenty, hundred dollar bills; slowly, licking his thumb between each one. I signed the bill of sale and the Scatt was his.

"Now, I'd like to see the sail and whatever else goes with her," he said. So we drove to Sunshine and I motored him out to Crow in our dinghy. But before we left the motel, I poked my head out the door and looked both ways—scanned the property for suspicious-looking characters—and on the way out in the boat, I moved the wad of dough from my pants right side pocket to my left rear (which had a flap on it with a button), and finally to the left-hand pocket of my flannel shirt (also buttonable), where it felt more secure. It was misting slightly, but Mr. Scott just sat there in his shirt sleeves, beaming, his eyes glancing from one scene to another as if he'd never been in a boat before, or in such a pretty place, or among such pleasant and jovial people.

"How do you do?" he said to Lucy, grasping her strongly by the hand. "Beautiful house you have here. Beautiful island."

It was lunch time. Mr. Scott allowed that he was ravenous. He ate two turkey sandwiches and drank three glasses of milk, and after coffee and cookies and some plums, we dug out the sail. We pulled it down from on top of the closet where it had been sitting for almost two years, carried it to the nearest ledge and spread it out. Ants. Millions of ants took off in every direction. I rushed back into the house to find a broom while Mr. Scott laughed and laughed in between exclamations about what good shape the sail was in. What must he have expected, I wondered, that made him so enthusiastic about everything he saw? And if he'd expected so little, why had he bothered to come?

He took everything, including the old life preservers we'd had since the tourist days and the original mattresses—faded canvas covers glued forever now to the lumpy, crumbling, mildewed foam rubber. He took the charts, most of them so hopelessly water-stained as to be indecipherable. He took the pots and the pans and the kitchen silver, most of it purchased secondhand twenty-five years ago. He took the galvanized pump with its hose and its rags, a boxful of rusty tools, the compass, the parallel rules.

"Is there a foghorn?" he asked.

"Only this," I replied, holding up the conch shell we'd found on the beach on Sanibel Island in Florida twenty-four years ago, hacksawed the end off of and used as our sea trumpet ever since. "And that doesn't go." That and the captain's cap Mama Reeves had given me when we set out from Mantoloking on our maiden voyage were the only things from the Scatt we kept. The cap was torn and stained and sewn up with sail thread, but the Captain's insignia was still there and the visor still shone. The shell was unchanged.

The Scatt too was pretty much unchanged since the day we got her. But no. That wasn't really true. Mr. Scott was getting a much better boat than the one we had bought. He wouldn't have to bore holes in the keel at random and pump in white lead. She wouldn't fill up when they put her in the water, not if he caulked and puttied and maybe refastened a little. And he wouldn't have to sleep at night with his arm hanging over onto the floor so that when the water hit his hand he would know it was time to get up and pump. Had he expected a wreck like this, though? A floating cocktail lounge that nobody in his right mind would consider taking out of the bay?

"Where are you going to keep the Scatt?" Lucy asked him.

"Portland," he said. "Got a daughter there. Be a good excuse to visit."

"But you live in California. What part?"

"Riverside," he said, "where the worst smog is. But I get a lot of time off."

"What do you do?" I asked, wondering why I hadn't inquired before.

"I'm on an oil tanker. Go back and forth to Alaska. Six months on, six months off."

"What's your job?" I said.

"Oh, I'm the captain."

So that was it. His wife had a harpsichord. That was her love. What he wanted was a boat—one big enough to live aboard. He'd been brought up in Maine. Spending his summers in Portland would be like going home.

"So you're going to sail her to Portland?" Lucy said, containing her disbelief admirably.

"Hope to," he said and grinned. "Have to see what sort of shape she's in first."

Mr. Scott was puttying an upper seam when I saw him about a week later. He'd already caulked and painted the bottom. He was smiling more broadly than ever, if that was possible. "She's in better condition than I thought," he said. "Pretty good, considering." He pointed out a few places where he'd had to refasten a butt joint. He'd taken off the garboards, he told me, and found the ribs to be sound. He'd tightened down the steering with a new fitting over the shaft, greased her, replaced the pins in the rudder, and when he turned the wheel, it spun. "That'll build up the old arms—holding that barn door shut when she blows."

I guess probably, I thought, wondering what other miracles he had in mind.

A few days later I was by again. There was a three-speed bicycle leaning up against the cradle. "Got a visitor?" I asked, nodding in its direction.

"No," he said. "I got tired of paying for the car, so I turned her in and bought that." And then he told me what he'd done, exactly, and I realized for the first time that Mr. Scott was a man one could reasonably approach with feelings of awe. He had turned his car in at the airport in Trenton, hitchhiked the ten miles to Ellsworth, bought this bicycle at Western Auto and ridden it the forty-some hilly miles to Stonington, not having been on a bicycle for years. Sixty-seven years old, going on sixteen.

From then on I knew there was no limit to what Mr. Scott could do. And there wasn't. He built himself a dinghy. He recanvassed the cabin and the decks, and I couldn't tell whether he'd butted the edges up or gone under things, his workmanship was so fine. He painted the hull and cabintop blue, Endeavor Blue, as we'd always had it, her decks light gray and the rest of her a shining white, inside and out. He took the engine out of her and replaced it with a secondhand, six-horse Evinrude. He wasn't planning to motor her, he said, except in and out of harbors. I remembered all the days we'd thought the same. I remembered the idea I'd had at one time of fitting out the Scatt with oversized oar-locks and huge oars, and saying goodbye to the problems of power forever, but I'd never had the nerve to do it. Even the oldest and worst and least dependable of engines gave one a sense of security that oars or an outboard did not. What would he do in big seas off a lee shore, say? What would he do if the Scatt opened up on him? But I answered my own question before I asked it. I'd learned some things over the years, even if I didn't always put them into practice.

He had bought a fifty-pound fisherman's anchor and what looked like a hundred-foot coil of one-inch nylon rope. The rigging was new, the sail firmly patched. He had the old gaff lashed to the top of the cabin. Eventually he'd restore that, too. Three weeks and he was ready to go, and looking younger and more rugged and jovial than ever. We were planning to see him off, but we didn't. He left in the fog one morning. No one we spoke to actually saw him go. And so we missed him. I was pretty sure the Scatt wouldn't open up on him the first time a good wind hit. I was pretty sure, too, that compared to us—or anyone—he had superior powers of coping, unplumbed depths of know-how, cunning and sufficient strength—as befitted a lonely Odysseus.

I never thought that I'd be happy selling the Scatt. But I was. Almost as happy as Lucy and I felt the day we first saw her, sitting in her cradle in that boatyard in Mantoloking, waiting for us.

EPILOGUE

Why, you might ask, was not the Scatt kept in the family? If I didn't want to deal with her anymore, couldn't we have put her away for some future time when the energies of Paul or Patrick, or someone else, moved in that direction? Given her antiquity, her semi-historic place in the history of wooden boats, weren't we foolish as well as ungrateful to have let her go? Perhaps, but this was not 1952. Paul and Patrick did not have their summers free. Even more to the point, we had entered the age of fiberglass. A wooden boat was an anachronism, a relic from another time. For the money it cost me to keep the Scatt for one year, I could buy a fiberglass sloop. Something small, easy to handle. A daysailer like the White Seal, only impervious to decay.

And that's just what we did. Within a week of selling the Scatt, we were the proud owners of Harold, a nineteen-foot O'Day Mariner. It had come without a name, and I had christened it with a name that was as unsuitable as I could think of both to show the seaman's then-traditional contempt for fiberglass and to appease any spirits from the vasty deep that might be jealous of so swift a shift of allegiances. We had been fortunate. Harold was sitting under a tarp in Burnt Cove Boatyard; his owner lived in western Maine and was more interested in canoes.

"See if she'll take eight hundred dollars," I said to the proprietress of the boatyard, who had the owner's wife on the phone. The boat was priced at one-thousand five-hundred dollars.

"She says she will."

"Doesn't she want to check with her husband?" I answered, too stunned to play cagey.

"Nope."

So Harold took his place in the family.

For years we wanted no other boat. Harold not only sailed well and fitted us all into the cockpit for picnics and even short cruises, he cost nothing at all. We hauled him out ourselves on Crow Island without so much as the benefit of a cradle (he was a centerboard), and we did not even paint his bottom. In August, when he started to get slimy, we beached him out and scrubbed him off with sand. It was all very much a matter of pride. My pride, that is. I was getting back my due.

And then in April of 1985 Paul found us Buttercup. We'd been talking about how nice it would be to get a real cruising boat, something we could sail to Roque Island in, or even further. Paul and Jennifer had finished their house (more or less) and had blessed us all with their firstborn, Marisol (sea plus sun). Were we secretly desirous of widening our horizons? Patrick, a builder of other people's houses now and an off-and-on instructor with Outward Bound (which involved much coastal sailing in open boats), was also enthusiastic. Harold had served his purpose, but all of us were conscious of a lack.

"Let's buy her," said Lucy. (Among other things, she loved the name.) I needed no persuasion. For Buttercup was a catboat. A twenty-two foot fiberglass auxiliary (Marshall) catboat that looked new, had a roomy cabin with two double bunks, and was "fully found."

We were living in Maine year-round now, a couple of miles away from Paul and Jennifer, since I had taken early retirement. We had more need of a "real" boat. We could even afford one. And so we purchased Buttercup and prepared to relive the past.

Buttercup turned out to be a cream puff, just what the Scatt should have been. She was roomy, safe and dependable. What's more, she sailed well, even into the wind. Gaff-rigged, she carried as much sail as the Scatt had at the end. We cruised in her as far as Canada and enjoyed countless sailing picnics in her company; and I particularly loved taking her out in a blow, triplereefed, without worrying that I was going to break her mast. She never broke her mooring, or put herself up on the rocks, or failed in a crisis. She never even behaved in an unseemly manner.

So what's the matter with me? Why do I keep comparing her odiously to the Scatt?

The Scatt is ours no more. But we will survive. We have two fiberglass boats now, Buttercup and slimy-bottomed Harold. We are not exactly boat poor.

* * *

But what about the Scatt? What news? Did Mr. Scott ever make it to Portland? Are he and the Scatt even still around?

I don't know. I never wrote down Mr. Scott's address. Sometimes, when we pass the Portland exits on the turnpike, we are tempted to turn off and make for the waterfront; but we never have, and probably never will.

I do hope that wherever she is, she is well cared for. As long as her new owner does not decide to move to Sedgwick and moor the Scatt next to Buttercup in the Benjamin River, I would love to think that she has been perfectly restored. For a wooden boat is special. As long as a single original piece of her remains, she can be made new indefinitely.

LaVergne, TN USA
08 February 2011
215659LV00001B/83/A